DE(

Concepts in
String Playing

Concepts in String Playing

Reflections by Artist-Teachers at the Indiana University School of Music

Edited by

Murray Grodner

 Indiana University Press
BLOOMINGTON AND LONDON

Manufactured in the United States of America
Library of Congress Cataloging in Publication Data
Main entry under title:

Concepts in string playing.

   1. Stringed instruments, Bowed—Instruction and study. I. Grodner,
Murray.
MT259.C66   787'.01'071   78-13811
ISBN 0-253-18166-6   1 2 3 4 5 83 82 81 80 79

To the memory of David Dawson

Contents

Concepts in
String Playing

James Buswell IV

The Many Faces
of Musical Talent

"What a great talent! Such a pity that he has never been taught anything about music."

"This woman has some talent, but she has such difficulty in expressing what she feels."

"Now that is a wonderful natural talent, but there seems to be very little sensitivity."

"Here is a very hard worker who is an intelligent musician, but unfortunately he has no talent."

"This fellow has a lot of talent but seemingly no desire."

As comments such as these are bandied about by professionals and laymen, teachers and students—indeed by those who think of themselves as "talented" and by those who wish they were—the word *talent* becomes so hopelessly muddled that I feel inclined to dispense with it entirely. But then a new face emerges, with a musical utterance of peculiar strength, coherence, and beauty. Caught up in the fresh musical vision, and quite unconcerned with semantics, I find myself turning to a colleague and speaking of "talent." We all are guilty of forcing this vast, noble, and complex idea into our cramped mental sets and into our stale and convenient dichotomies.

Members of the musical fraternity are especially presumptuous in drawing sharp lines between what can and what cannot be taught, while students of early child development struggle to distinguish between innate and acquired skills, and the science that attempts to deal with these questions is in its own infancy. And who is to say that *talent* by definition must refer only to qualities that are inborn? It would seem that all our skills, even those we are most proud of having strenuously "acquired," are gifts bestowed by the Creator with or without human assistance.

3

It is decidedly not my intention here to deal with the age-old enigma of heredity versus environment as it pertains to musical talent. Rather I would like to share a few impressions, received during two decades of music making and only a very few years of teaching, that may serve to broaden and enrich the popular notions of musical talent. Surveying the fundamental areas of musical performance ability in a basically clinical manner, I find that as a teacher I can see each student's profile of assets and deficiencies more clearly, and therefore teach more effectively.

It would seem self-evident that musical talent appears in three distinct modes: the physical, the emotional, and the intellectual. Yet it always astonishes me to discover that many musicians habitually, and usually only semiconsciously, think of talent as belonging chiefly to only one of these areas. Let me introduce you somewhat humorously to three contrasting musical personalities. Partly because of their early training (musical and otherwise), their dramatic youthful impressions of genius, and the later development of their artistic identities (not necessarily self-imposed), each one has allowed his perception of talent to become warped in a different way. When such a bias announces itself only in casual conversation it is harmless enough. Too often, however, our biases influence and limit the clarity of our judgment when we attempt to perceive and evaluate talent in others.

Meet first a musician who may have spent some years teaching students of very modest technical abilities. Each time he has the pleasure of instructing a physically more responsive student, he is overwhelmed by the far greater ease with which this pupil acquires mechanical skills. He is a little impatient with colleagues whose pedagogical priorities emphasize understanding before doing. Very likely he will put enormous stock in the age at which a student commenced study and will discourage an older student who is trying to catch up. To his mind facility is always an asset and is in itself glorious. Often such a teacher suffers from some physical shortcoming in his own art; it may be serious or inconsequential, but he is acutely aware of it. We are always most impressed by those qualities we think we do not possess. We tend to presume that our own deficiencies are in the area of talent rather than effort.

Our second musician subscribes often and loudly to the conviction that to be moved is really all that matters in art. One of my earliest teachers used to put it very beautifully. "If I pay my five dollars for a concert, I will sit down in my seat and appreciate many things about an artist and admire what he can do. Or I may disapprove very much of his sense of style, find his musical taste offensive, and question his breeding. But if just once I do this . . . ," and at this point he would brush away an imaginary tear from his eye, "then I know that I have gotten my money's worth."

This musician rarely finds it possible to awaken a musical imagination. He tends to decide very early what are the emotional sensibilities of a student. If he finds them deficient he will try to paste on to the pupil's personality a collage of expressive gestures that he hopes will masquerade as genuine expression and hide what he considers a basic emptiness. He is always attracted by a sort of expressive *chutzpah* that he feels must be at the core of musical talent. If a student possesses this, he will be uncommonly indulgent with him and tolerate massive lapses in discipline, energy, or taste.

Finally, we must make the acquaintance of a musician who prizes most highly the student who thinks. He is unimpressed by strength or agility when it is uninformed. He is turned off by expressive urgency when it is not molded by a sense of style. He teaches largely by abstract principles and is impatient with the student who fails to grasp them. He may actually become suspicious of facility as an indication of shallowness. This type of musician has often become intellectually oriented later in life and has forgotten what he owes in his own art to his earlier, more intuitive training. He may be in fact or in self-image a "redeemed virtuoso," who stresses *ad nauseam* the supremacy of the composer and the selflessness of the performer.

I have intentionally exaggerated the idiosyncrasies of these three personalities for greater clarity and contrast. For pedagogical reasons it is important to differentiate the three areas in which talent manifests itself. When a teacher perceives a deficiency in a student's natural ability, it is crucial that the teacher decide where to focus his energies—on the mind, the body, or the spirit. Often we associate an ability with only one of these areas, when in fact it has physical, emotional, and mental components. For example, a student may be rich in one ability in its intellectual mode but be quite unable to demonstrate the corresponding emotional manifestation of this talent. It seems to me wrong to dismiss such a student as "untalented." Some weaknesses will respond to remediation much more willingly than others. But I refuse to allow the word *talent* to be defined as "that special composite of abilities that can never be taught." Too often we make no attempt to teach because although we appreciate the outward signs of a talent, we do not understand the inner workings of that gift. In the following pages I should like to go into some detail in dissecting and outlining some of the discrete strands of musical talent.

Excellent coordination is almost invariably thought of as a purely physical virtue. Even from a mechanical standpoint, coordination is compound in nature. Someone with good physical coordination is expected to learn quickly how to execute simultaneously two or more motions that ordinarily occur separately. Conversely, we may expect such a person to have little difficulty in separating motions that habitually occur together and perform them at different times and under different circumstances. These connecting and disconnecting aptitudes are not necessarily equal in one student's bag of "talents."

Many violin students struggle to develop the high degree of independence demanded of the two hands. A string player's hands usually do very different things, and at times they must feel exactly opposite sensations. If a student is very slow to learn such things, I may in exasperation come to regard him as uncoordinated. Then I will be surprised to discover that it is very natural for him to coordinate the unity of vibrato acceleration and increased bow speed in a good musical accent, and I find myself guilty of having made a hasty decision in just one small area of musical talent.

There are many other types of coordination crucial to the development of a performing artist. The precise coordination of ear perception, for example, wanders into a shadowy area between the physical and the mental. Many musical relatives such as velocity, volume, and amplitude or frequency of vibrato are mechanically or psychologically coupled in habitual combinations that must be uncoupled in order to realize artistic freedom and variety of color.

Before this uncoupling procedure can take place, the ear must be able to distinguish subtle changes in these variables.

The performer's mind has another complex coordinational responsibility in the heat of action. It must report on past events, monitor the present, and mold the future simultaneously. It has often been said that the musician with excellent intonation makes no fewer mistakes than one with just passable intonation. He simply reacts so quickly to his errors that he corrects them before most ears have noticed them. The greatest artist reacts also to the pleasing aspects of the past and responds with depth of feeling not only to what he has just done but also to what he has just heard. The performing musician must be both chef and gourmet. Reaction plays a variable role in, but is not the entirety of, the present in the ongoing musical stream. Superb attention and alertness join forces with carefully trained reflexes in the execution of each detail in the present.

Then there is the problem of anticipation. Many well-meaning conductors or accompanists seek to soothe or at least to impress the soloist with the words, "Now, please, be perfectly free, and whatever you do, I will follow you." I have gotten into the habit of replying, "If you follow me, that means you will be behind me, and that is not good enough."

Anticipation is more than a matter of ensemble with another musician. It is the total vision of the proportion and peculiar symmetries and asymmetries of each composition that a performer should enjoy, whether he plays alone or as a very small unit of an orchestra. I have worked with students who have outstanding reactive coordination but who anticipate poorly and are constantly being "blind-sided" by problems they never suspected. Peripheral vision is vital to the athlete; an important skill for the musician to cultivate is "peripheral hearing."

Often the psychological timing required in the training of fine mechanical coordination is very delicate. I will draw again on the omnipresent problem of playing in tune. As nearly as I can perceive it, the mind must perform the following gymnastics within an instant: A new note is about to be played. The mind's ear calls forth a precise image of what the new pitch should be, and the finger or hand sets up its own image of what the new note will feel like. At this point the mind dare not entertain the slightest doubt that the approaching maneuver will be successful, and the finger comes down or the hand moves with the utmost authority. Now the new note begins to sound, and the mind must execute a 180° turn in attitude. Complete confidence is replaced by deep suspicion. Before the mind is allowed to begin anticipating the next note, it must scrutinize intensely the note now sounding. If it proves even slightly false, the finger must react as violently as if it had touched the proverbial hot stove. But the reaction must not be one of repulsion but of a very specific directional attraction to a tonal center. Many quite sensitive students react to faulty intonation with a general vibrato, which creates a sort of smoke screen but no ultimate correction.

Like physical coordination, emotional coordination presents a compound problem. There are obviously times when an artist's emotions must flow quite directly into the physical execution of the composition he is performing. A short, accentuated chord such as that at the end of the Paganini Fifth Caprice provides a natural release of emotions that have built up and, we hope, have been carefully controlled throughout the piece. If the performance has gone well, the feeling of triumph and exhilaration can be channeled directly into the muscles to produce an appropriately aggressive exclamation point. If the performance has "bombed" (rarely are there mediocre renditions of this work), the accompanying sentiments of anger and frustration will cause the muscles to produce a very similar kind of chord.

There are many other occasions, however, in which the natural physical responses called forth by a certain highly appropriate emotion must be intercepted and cast aside in favor of a very different set of sensations. The desired sound will be produced although the emotion and the motion may seem strangely incongruous. Again, some students have a wonderful natural emotional flow but have great difficulty when the flow must be diverted. Others are very good at compartmentalizing the spirit and the body, but when the two are called upon to pull together, they seem quite baffled. Very often a poverty of emotion is mistaken for great physical control. The struggle between body and spirit is intrinsic to certain styles of art, and operates on both the physical and the metaphysical level.

Most laypersons find it very difficult to conceive of the amount of energy expended by the musical performer. In scholarly pursuits a consistently high level of mental energy is expected, but the physical and emotional energy levels may remain quite low. In athletics the physical energy put forth is very high, but only a very few sports demand the level of mental and emotional intensity required of the artist in the heat of performance. The combination of energies expended during a two-hour recital add up to more than the equivalent of a full day's work.

The energy output is not always obvious. Somewhere deep in the laws of esthetics lies the principle that a difficult task made to appear easy is in itself beautiful. This is decidedly not the highest form of beauty, although certain periods of art have seemed to think so. To appear godlike is not nearly as beautiful as to reflect God's beauty. Still, most great artists do attempt to disguise to some degree the physical effort that goes into the execution of their designs. This disguise requires great control, and control requires additional energy.

Energy potential is definitely a significant part of talent. The physical energy demanded in musical performance can be thought of as the proper use of tension. Tension becomes an evil only when it turns mindlessly against itself and prevents action. This will be discussed further when we consider agility.

One facet of physical energy in performance that must be carefully cultivated in most students is the ability very suddenly to augment or diminish the amount of local muscular power being applied. On any instrument it is difficult to control the sudden release of tension required in a subito piano. A real sforzando on a sustained note is more complex. The muscles must wait until the last possible instant to build up the high level of energy needed for the sforzando event. If the tension increases too soon, a self-destructive tightness occurs because the tension is static. After the sforzando itself, in order for the note to endure beautifully, there must be an equally sudden reduction of energy in the musculature. Many students who have plenty of natural physical energy are totally unaccustomed to the discipline of using it in sudden, precise bursts.

Great physical energy does not presuppose great mental energy. When I observe a musician possessed of superior mental energy, I am always struck by his or her inventiveness and imagination. The mind of such an artist keeps poking around in the mass of experiential data and comes up with the most extraordinary parallels of idea and of sensation. A piece of music springs to life in his mind, animated by all manner of imagery, some of it useful in teaching, and some of it very private and communicable only through the medium of the music itself. If imagination and mental energy are not synonymous, they certainly are closely related.

The energetic musical mind is always eager to perceive and to illuminate connecting fibers between the musical and the extramusical worlds. Some musicians would have it that these fibers are of only coincidental interest, and do not lie close to the heart of musical experience. I would dispute that. Art must spring from both the theoretical and the visceral, from idea and from sensation; it must create new worlds while reflecting the world around it if it is to be more than just an exclusive intellectual game. But then, if the phenomenon of human life is presumed to be an intriguing and rather perverse accident, the lines of the argument must be drawn much farther back into the areas of metaphysics and religion. The reader may puzzle over the conceit of even mentioning such heavy subjects within the context of a discussion of talent. I am only bent on indicating here that one's view of the nature of musical talent and, indeed, the nature of music itself ultimately depends on how one sees human nature—what it is and why it is. What for one person is a tangent is for another a root.

A high level of emotional energy is crucial for the performing artist. I often remind my students that it is not enough that they feel something deeply. They must also be able to project that feeling to every member of the audience. A performer is really a very peculiar fellow, in that he is not satisfied until he has laid bare his deepest feelings to perfect strangers, in the hope that they will experience them also.

It is partly for this reason that most artists have an intense desire to be alone or to be with only their closest friends immediately following a performance. The need for privacy is very strong in the wake of the extreme openness that is essential to a powerful musical utterance. The usual post-concert reception comes as a flagrant violation of this need. A leisurely meal after the concert with a few friends is so much more salutary, not only because it helps to replenish the body's depleted resources but also because the artist can gradually restore and compose himself behind the more impersonal formality of eating.

, We are always impressed by individuals who seem to have an almost boundless capacity for work. We marvel at their "energy" and use the word loosely. But this kind of energy is also a legitimate form of talent. It is useless and absurd to keep wondering why "exceptionally talented" people often seem to be lazy. It seems natural to me that gifted young people develop many skills with relatively little effort and have little reason to acquire the additional qualities of perseverance and endurance. Those who must struggle to mine and refine their talents soon develop an enormous capacity for work, which may become their greatest talent.

Agility is more difficult to define than *energy*, even in the physical realm. The word is often used to mean simply quickness of reflex. As such, agility is a gift that has certainly been distributed among humankind in very unequal portions. Still, one's natural reflexes can be seriously hampered by several factors. Nervous tension and fatigue have well-known, detrimental effects on the reflexes. Whereas alertness properly understood is a virtue, some students' attempts at alertness bring on physical tension that actually in- creases reaction time. Alertness is a mental quality that can be studiously cultivated. But to be physically alert is to be totally re- laxed. I have observed quite a few eager students under pressure to do their best whose reflexes appear to be very slow only because their attempts at readiness and poise create great physical and psychic tension, binding the muscles and prohibiting quick response.

The physical agility demanded of the musical performer requires more than just quickness of reflex. A broader definition is "the ability to achieve maximum effect with minimum effort." Many string players bemoan their lack of left-hand velocity and quickness and assume that it stems from some inborn sluggishness, or look in vain for some magical exercise that will increase fluency. Often they mindlessly expect their fingers to perform superfluous activities and to exaggerate many simple motions, thus creating useless labor.

Economy of effort is basic to the performing arts, both practically and esthetically, and native awareness of this principle is an impor- tant aspect of talent. Precisely for this reason the gifted musician often appears nonchalant or excessively casual. It may be years before such a performer realizes that economy of effort on stage must be coupled with thorough preparation and total emotional commitment. Sometimes a young artist already realizes this, and the teacher may be guilty of confusing a legitimate mark of talent with a lack of seriousness.

Alertness is only one aspect of mental agility. An alert musician notices things. To notice intelligently is to discriminate between subtle shades of color. An agile mind will then be able to decide quickly which shade to choose. Finally, if new circumstances render the earlier decision inappropriate, agility manifests itself in the ability to adjust quickly.

Let us suppose that in a performance of chamber music a collaborator executes an exquisite diminuendo. First, I must be listening with sufficient intensity and depth to notice that a diminuendo is taking place. Then I must be discriminating enough to perceive the slope of this nuance and other characteristics, such as subtle accompanying changes in vibrato and bow speed. Instantly I should be able to decide just what nuance on my part will complement the ongoing diminuendo of my colleague. Merely to mirror him is often not sufficient or even appropriate. During these musical maneuvers I may discover that because of the peculiar acoustics of the auditorium the proper balance among voices has been disrupted, and I must adjust my level of volume accordingly—but smoothly, not abruptly. Among artists of great and well-cultivated talent, these subtle sensitivities and nuances take place with incredible swiftness. The intimacy of communication that exists is really quite startling.

Musical talent commands the attention of the listener from the very first note. The mood of the composition is projected immediately, and emotional agility allows the performer to lose himself totally and unself-consciously in the music. And when the mood suddenly changes in the course of the composition, that talent permits him to reflect and project that change with gusto. Happily such agility of spirit is not found only in people of volatile temperament. In fact, the disciplined indulgence of emotions in a musical recital provides the healthy artistic spirit with a kind of release that may reinforce a calm and even-tempered disposition.

One of the most obvious manifestations of musical talent is a good sense of rhythm. This means much more than accuracy in reproducing the notation in a musical score. What is really meant is a good sense of timing, a sensitivity to the creative relationship of time to sound.

It has been observed many times that the body's mechanisms of circulation and respiration give to every creature a certain sense of rhythm. One unmistakable sign of musical talent is the early development of a comfortable synchronization of the rhythm of breathing with the rhythm of the music being played. For the singer or wind player, this facility should develop regardless of talent. But even among these musicians, for whom the breath is the very conveyor of their art, talented students will quickly discover breathing patterns that enhance the musical line, while their less fortunate colleagues need to be coached phrase by phrase. Whereas the latter breathe because they must, gifted students breathe when the music must breathe.

Unhappily many students of the keyboard or stringed instruments may study for years before discovering that breathing has anything to do with musical rhythm. A despairing teacher may plead with such a student to "sing on your instrument." The teacher knows exactly what he means. But the student may be unable to translate the teacher's words into, "Breathe when you play, and allow your music to breathe freely and with regular pulsation."

Without ever developing a sensitivity to meter or beat, most people develop a sense of rhythm within the fabric of their daily lives. Certain kinds of routines are powerful tools for getting a long task accomplished, just as a repetitive cadence in music can build a great climax. But the same routine or rhythmic gesture, if carried out mindlessly and past the point of its usefulness, turns into tedium or annoyance. In some cultures more than in others the way a person walks and the cadence of his speech grow out of a very personal sense of rhythm. In midwestern American English the prevailing spoken language patterns seem to avoid rhythmic vitality at all costs.

The young musician who cultivates a talent for rhythmic expression begins by learning to measure time. He then learns to relate measured time to sound. At some point he becomes powerfully aware that time is never suspended in music—not during rests or fermatas, or between movements, or even, in a sense, between compositions on a program. He may develop special skills for handling complex subdivisions of meter. Or he may acquire an exceptionally fine tempo memory. But these are auxiliary talents, useful but secondary. It is the continuous awareness of ongoing time and the need to organize it in some meaningful way that lies at the bottom of rhythmic talent.

Nature provides within us and outside us a means of organization in the alternation of strong and weak beats within the flow of time. An immature musician will perceive these beats as the essence of rhythm just as anyone may equate the ticks of a clock with time itself. But the great artist always feels the flow of time in between and through the beats, and he molds this flow to create a line. Then the musical event becomes a living thing, accurate in its structure, flexible in its development, and inventive in its proportions.

The musician gifted with a good sense of timing will also become a bit of a psychologist. He will learn to put himself in the shoes of his listeners, and to become acutely aware of how their perception of the sequence of events will differ from his. For the listener the composition is always being created as it is being played, and it must contain a range of events from the quite predictable to the totally unexpected. As an artisan the performer must practice the execution of each composition exhaustively to assure that everything will be more than predictable, almost automatic. Then as an artist he has the spiritually difficult task of recapturing his naivete by literally pretending that he is creating the work for the first time as he is playing it. The musical gestures that surprise the audience must also surprise him at the same instant, or the performance will be unconvincing and stillborn. It must become impossible for the audience to imagine that this piece of art has ever happened before. In the same way, the performer should feel that each performance is the first one, unrelated and quite incomparable to any other.

A young musician who enjoys this capacity will show little or no nervousness or stage fright. It is not just that he is self-assured or that he mercifully lacks self-consciousness. He actually perceives himself as a part of the audience looking on at the unfolding of a masterpiece. Since the performance is unique, there is nothing to compare it with, not even the ideal in the mind of the performer, because the ideal and the reality have become one. There is then no fear of falling short of a norm or an ideal, and therefore no cause for nervousness. After the performance, the ideal and the reality will often diverge in the artist's memory, and he can then become his own best critic.

It is the last of the five quotations at the opening of this essay that appears to me the most absurd. I suppose that it would be possible for a person to possess all the talents discussed to this point and still not demonstrate the quality we call "desire." But such a person has never crossed my path. In my experience desire is usually the foundation of the richly talented musician. It would seem to me that in any vocation the love of what one is doing and the need to do it are the greatest of all talents. The student who is accused of having "talent" without "desire" may possess some physical skills that are spectacular in themselves but are rarely integrated with corresponding intellectual and emotional strengths.

The love of one's metier is ideally nourished by the growth of ability and proficiency. The mastery of a stringed instrument involves an unusually long gestation period even for the student of many talents. Desire that is not intense or not fortified by patience can be extinguished easily. But when desire burns brightly and accelerates the development of all skills, it is a beautiful thing to observe. It inspires the teacher and makes his task much simpler. On the occasions when I have had the pleasure of working with a student who has such a high level of desire, I have been convinced that this quality is talent in its purest form, capable of rising above a multitude of handicaps.

As with the other varieties of musical talent looked at earlier, this gift seems to have physical, intellectual, and spiritual manifestations that need to be distinguished. They do not necessarily appear in equal proportions in each personality. The two sensations—one tactile, the other aural—of producing free and open vibration and of receiving beauty of sound in the ear are quite separate delights. The very simple physical desire to produce and to hear a beautiful sound can be aroused early in a student's development, but if it is stimulated late it always seems to suffer from an accompanying self-consciousness. For a violinist the sensation of feeling the vibrations of wood against shoulder or of horsehair against gut may become a source of pleasure at any level of consciousness. If this love of sonority becomes narcissistic, full artistic maturity is impossible. Quite a few famous singers blessed with outstanding natural instruments provide ample illustration.

Intellectually, the student of great desire is eager to comprehend and control all possible variables of musical expression. It is fascinating just to watch such a student listening to a concert. He may or may not be enjoying the performance, but he constantly scrutinizes and analyzes every musical gesture of the performer and of the composer, adding each piece of information to his own artistic personality. His face reflects first the instantaneous recognition and appreciation of something beautiful, but this is immediately followed by a questioning expression: "How did he do that (performer or composer)? What variable did he manipulate to achieve that effect? Under what circumstances would that be appropriate?" And most important, "How can I make that happen on my instrument?" For such a talent the musical imagination is not limited by the instrument the student plays. He listens to all forms of his art with equal curiosity, recognizing that the possibility of inspiration is as universal as the language of music itself.

The emotional component of desire is usually described as the need for self-expression. Certainly this need is present in every sincere artist. Performing musicians, like many of their fellow human beings, find the kaleidoscope of their experiences powerfully stimulating, and the emotions aroused find natural outlet in their profession. I have already referred to the peculiar proclivity of performers to share the full intensity of their feelings with anyone who will listen. Other people may feel this urge on isolated occasions but rarely feel free to indulge themselves. Artists are driven by this urge day after day, and society sanctions their self-indulgence.

But the greatest artists are consumed by a desire for expression whose object is more than self. The concert musician must submerge himself deeply in the formal principles and the implied emotions of the composition he is about to illuminate. (I scrupulously avoid the highly misleading word *interpret*.) He may dig into the mind of the composer. Sometimes this birthplace of a composition turns out to be a palace full of treasures, or it may prove to be a vulgar and tawdry hovel. A lovely flower may be carefully cultivated in one or rise from the debris of the other. Still, a performer's immediate responsibility is to the flower.

One hopes that both the creation and the re-creation will be greater than either the creator or the re-creator. The progression of "desire" in a talented performing musician grows naturally from the affection for the instrument that is his tool (physical manifestation), through an affection for the composition that constitutes his medium (intellectual manifestation), and culminates in an affection for God Himself, who is in full the Creator (spiritual manifestation). Natural affections for composers and for fellow performers provide rich inspiration for this process, but these affections are by their very nature secondhand.

The true artist will choose his composition because it in turn illuminates something that is true. As he stands on stage, he will not be pointing at himself, or at the composer, or even directly at the composition. He will use his own hand unashamedly to point through the transparency of the composition to what he sees of permanent value beyond.

Josef Gingold

Advice to Aspiring
Young Symphony Musicians

Some sixty years ago, the basic training for the orchestra violinist consisted of playing in small ensembles. Those were the days when hotels would engage anything from a piano trio to a "six-piece" ensemble consisting of piano, cello, three violins, and double bass playing arrangements of overtures, operatic fantasies, waltzes, and occasionally a slow movement from a symphonic work.

There was also the silent moving picture. Every theater employed from two to eight musicians. When the large, so-called palace theaters were built, the orchestras, with a full complement, would employ from thirty-five to fifty musicians. These were the exception to the rule since only the large cities, such as New York, Boston, Chicago, Detroit, or Los Angeles, offered such grandiose musical fare. I cite these two examples because as a training school for future symphony players, theater ensembles, in their day, were the best possible education. It taught the players to be alert, improved their sightreading, and in the case of the smaller ensembles, made them listen constantly to their own playing.

I should also mention stage productions of musicals, for they served a good purpose, in a way. Playing the same show night after night gave the musician the important experience of never taking his eyes off the baton, since no two performances were ever alike, but other than that they added little to his future as a symphony player.

Then along came radio, which for years employed thousands of musicians, since all programs were broadcast live. This opened a new field, for with the advent of talking pictures, thousands of musicians employed in the moving picture theaters were thrown out of work. The musicians employed by a large network in New York, for example, had to be the best all-around players one could find anywhere. The radio orchestra was by no means a training school, because the networks sought and employed experienced craftsmen. One had to be a "jack of all trades" when it came to handling the required repertoire.

In my own case, for example, as a member of the NBC staff from 1937 to 1943, on a typical musical Sunday I might be on the air at 8:00 A.M. playing music by Beethoven, Mozart, Haydn, or Tchaikovsky in a piano trio. After the broadcast, I would dash into another studio to rehearse with the Primrose String Quartet, until air time from 10:30 to 11:00. Then to a jazz orchestra, which broadcast from 12:30 until 1:00. At 5:00 P.M., the climax of the week, a concert with Arturo Toscanini! Or should I say the fulfillment of a lifetime.

In New York and Chicago, there existed and still exist two excellent training orchestras for future professional symphony artists: the National Orchestral Society of New York, conducted for years by Chalmers Clifton, and then by Leon Barzin; and the Civic Orchestra of Chicago, under Eric De Lemarter, which functioned to provide musicians for major orchestras. These bodies read music and performed several concerts annually, giving young players a basic foundation of orchestral playing. Some of the larger conservatories had orchestras in which students gained experience. In its early years (1925–30), Curtis Institute had an orchestra that might stand comparison with the major ensembles. Its conductors were Artur Rodzinski, and after his resignation, none other than Fritz Reiner! Juilliard also boasted a fine ensemble, under Albert Stoessel, and some of its graduates occupied leading positions in the orchestra field. Unlike the situation at present, college and university orchestras were not on a comparable level with the conservatory products. (Since then some notable universities have music departments that rival the better-known conservatories, and their recent graduates have found places in the major orchestras of the world, including even first-chair positions.) Curtis and Juilliard both set high standards, and when their graduates began infiltrating the leading symphony positions and ranks, the orchestra sound plus the technical brilliance reached new heights of orchestral performance.

Auditions in those days consisted mainly of a prepared solo piece, a movement of a concerto, for example; and for the rest of the tryout, the emphasis was on sightreading. It was in this category that many promising players failed the exam, which was given by the conductor with the assistance of the section leader (with whom the conductor consulted at times).

Within the past fifteen years or so, a new system of auditioning has been instituted and is followed by all orchestras. American musicians realized that a talented instrumentalist, who possessed great technical, tonal, and musical qualities, could, if given the time to prepare his individual orchestral parts, become an asset to their respective organizations. Conductors became interested primarily in first-class instrumentalists, and a new set of standards and demands came into being, which were unheard of in years gone by. For example, for an opening in the first violin section of a major orchestra, the following repertoire might be asked of a candidate:

Solo works: Bach—Adagio and Fugue, or two contrasting movements of a partita; Mozart—Concerto No. 5 (Joachim cadenza) or a standard concerto by Mendelssohn, Tchaikovsky, or Brahms.
Orchestral excerpts: Beethoven—Symphonies Nos. 3, 7, 9; Beethoven—Leonore Overture No. 3; Brahms—Symphonies Nos. 2, 4; Strauss—*Don Juan*; Mozart—Symphony No. 39; Bruckner—Symphony No. 7.

By the time of this writing, 1978, a great change had taken place in the number of string players who apply for positions in symphony orchestras. In the 1950s there was a dearth of string players, and conductors were combing the field to find suitable performers to fill vacancies. In the last twenty-five years, we seem to have overproduced both in quantity and, yes, in quality, the number of aspiring young people seeking careers in orchestras. As a result, when two or three openings occur, sixty or more players apply. Two years ago, one of our major orchestras announced a vacancy in the *second violin* section, seventh stand—the requirements being the first movement of the Brahms Violin Concerto, the Bach Chaconne, and the Mozart Concerto No. 5 from the solo literature, and ten difficult orchestral excerpts. Thirty-five violinists auditioned for this one opening, and the person chosen, a splendid fiddler whom I happened to know, was overjoyed at having been selected. Sixty years ago he might have pursued a solo career.

For the audition, the player prepares himself or is aided by a teacher, if he still is in his student years, and constantly wonders, "What are they looking for in my playing?" Well, most of the

committees listening to the applicants are musicians of the orchestra
chosen by their colleagues, and they are looking for *excellent instrumental playing*. They usually judge that by the solo repertoire. I
would say they are looking for fine tone quality, good intonation,
good rhythm, well-articulated technical passages, and intelligent
musicianship. The individual must rate himself on these qualities.
Better still, before the audition, use a tape recorder and listen to
yourself carefully. Criticize, play again, find out where the weak
spots are. Then, play for your colleagues and your teacher. Do not
make the mistake of leaving your practice room and going directly to
the audition without this preparation. The musical excerpts in Exx.
1–8 might be of some help to those who hope to audition for symphony jobs.

Ex. 1.   Beethoven, Symphony No. 3, *Allegro
con brio*.

Ex. 2.   Beethoven, Symphony No. 3, *Marcia
funebre, Adagio assai*.

Ex. 3. Beethoven, Symphony No. 3, last
movement, *Allegro molto.*

Ex. 4. Beethoven, Symphony No. 3, last
movement.

Ex. 5. Beethoven, Symphony No. 9, third movement, *Adagio molto e cantabile*.

Ex. 6. Beethoven, Leonore Overture, No. 3.

VIOLINO 1.

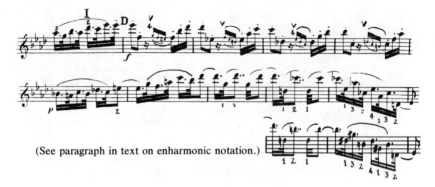

(See paragraph in text on enharmonic notation.)

Ex. 7.   Mozart, Symphony No. 39, second
movement, *Andante con moto.*

Ex. 8.   Strauss, *Don Juan.*

Once you have been accepted into a major orchestra, you will have to accommodate your personal playing to the musical surroundings. To begin with, be well prepared with the music at hand before each rehearsal; practice your own part with the same care for details as for a solo recital. *Never* take your eyes off the conductor, and cooperate at all times with your section leader. Listen carefully, not only to yourself but also to your stand partner and to the entire ensemble. Never force your tone even in *ff* passages.

The vibrato is one of the strongest assets in your instrumental makeup. Use it! It will add to the sound of the entire orchestra and give you much joy when you know that you are producing a beautiful tone. Use a lot of bow when the score calls for energetic playing. Watching the concertmaster at such times is most helpful.

Enharmonic translation is a valuable skill for an orchestral player. Our early education, good as it may be, has certain drawbacks. One of them is that it fails to train students to recognize symbols such as a succession of flats or double flats and immediately translate them for their instrumental comfort. The words *to, two,* and *too* are all pronounced alike even though they have different meanings; so it is with certain notes or intervals. The passage in Ex. 9 may look forbidding at first glance, but it is a C major scale!

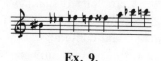

Ex. 9.

The symphonies of Bruckner are perhaps the best examples of the need to cultivate the art of enharmonic translation. Space does not permit more than the few bars from his Seventh Symphony shown in Ex. 10. Similar problems arise from time to time, but with daily rehearsals, concerts, experience, *and* continued study, it becomes second nature to resolve these difficulties.

Ex. 10. Bruckner, Symphony No. 7, second
movement, *Adagio*.

Having played in three major orchestras for a total of twenty-five years, I feel rewarded by the great conductors, soloists, and colleagues with whom I have had the good fortune to be associated. Playing under Toscanini and Szell was as valuable an education as studying with the finest violin teachers.

Playing the great works of the symphonic literature is an exhilarating experience and a most beautiful outlet for one's musical talent. When playing the "Eroica" or the Ninth Symphony, each performance will seem like the first one to you, so great is the creativity of Beethoven, the Shakespeare of music. With each playing, you will find new beauties and new problems to conquer; and these compositions are just a small part of the enormous repertoire—classic, Romantic, impressionistic, and contemporary—awaiting you.

Approach your work with love and enthusiasm.

Murray Grodner

The Double Bass —
A String Instrument

Having the privilege of being editor of this book has allowed me to read my colleagues' thoughts on string playing and music making before having to finalize my own contribution to this book. It has been inspiring, reinforcing, and enlightening to read all their views, which represent such a broad spectrum on the teaching and playing of music (on stringed instruments). I parenthesize "on stringed in-struments" because so much of what they say applies to teaching and music making on any instrument.

Most meaningful for me, as a bassist, is to find that these ideas correspond to and reinforce my own attitudes on performance. I have spent most of my playing and teaching years in very close musical association with violinists, violists, and cellists. During my twenty-two years at Indiana University I have been the only double bass instructor, and that has certainly created a much closer rela-tionship with other string players than I might have enjoyed as an orchestral bassist.

Other roads that life has led me down have also resulted in this type of association, which is not a usual one for a double bassist. For example, I spent two years of my military service as the only bass in a chamber orchestra of twenty-seven players. When I was initially assigned to this unusual unit, the group had only nine persons. It was in its formative stages and was inactive, awaiting the assignment and arrival of sufficient numbers and types of instruments to begin its official activities.

That original group consisted primarily of violinists and violists plus a pianist. They were all fine musicians, members of professional quartets and of several distinguished radio symphony orchestras.

They were very eager to do some playing, and of course chamber music was the only likely medium, but there was no cellist. Naturally when I was asked if I would like to try the cello parts on the bass, I jumped at the chance, for it was an unusual opportunity to play works by masters who otherwise wrote little or nothing for the double bass in small chamber ensembles. By playing an octave higher when possible and staying very "tuned in" to the practices of performance used by those I was playing with, I consciously and instinctively began to become "a string player."

As the only bassist after the group was formed, and having superb string players, wiser and more mature than I to learn from and blend with, I developed a consciousness of ensemble playing that has been invaluable to my total musical development and attitude toward the double bass. It eventually made me realize why it has taken the bass longer than the other strings to develop to a level of performance standards equal to theirs. Our poverty of literature, lack of attention paid to the bass outside the orchestral ensemble, and the archaic and unscientific method books written by probably very talented but unscientific teachers of the late nineteenth and early twentieth centuries have all resulted in our second- and third-class citizenship within the string family. With the coming of a more intellectual approach to pedagogy by men like Frederick Zimmermann and the success of contemporary virtuosi like Gary Karr and Ludwig Streicher, there was suddenly a realization of what bass playing could and should be, and that teaching needed to be an organized intellectual science, not just an instinctive passing-on of traditions.

Still vivid in my mind is the situation in New York when I was a student. There were "camps" of students. The camp you belonged to was determined by the teacher you studied with and his approach to sound and performance. It was not an interplay but more of a friendly polarization. Although traces of this era linger on, today there are regional conferences, bringing together teachers and students interested in each other and seeking to learn what is going on outside their own particular learning circle or class. In a way, perhaps we double bassists are doing more "reaching out" and "tuning in" than are the other string players and teachers. However, their heritage of pedagogy and literature automatically binds them in closer communication than we have ever had. Their method and etude books, written by truly great pedagogues; the great master-works for their instruments; their multitude of great performers, documented from the inception of recorded sound—all allow a communication that we are now only starting to develop.

At this point I have several concerns about where we are going as teachers and performers on the double bass. One is this same matter of communication. In our numerous efforts to achieve it through conferences, special schools, and recordings of solo double bass literature, we are inadvertently losing contact with other string players and their progress in music making and teaching. No orchestral instrument can become an entity unto itself. We must all work in full realization of what is going on in the world of music, but we must move with the family from which we came to prevent our falling behind, as we have in the past, or becoming insulated, polarized, or isolated in the future.

I would find it tragic if my students had no interest in attending the master classes of other members of the string faculty. The art and science of making music are too complex and vast for any one person to have it all figured out. Going to a master class given by a piano teacher and learning one thing about music you never realized before is an experience that may never be duplicated, for we all have different ways of expressing ideas. Understanding does not come from hearing an idea or a thought expressed, but from hearing that thought expressed in a manner that communicates the idea clearly to you. Often a student will report that he has learned something "new" I thought I had already taught him, but apparently it did not take hold in the same manner as it did in someone else's master class. Another student who had attended the same lecture may come back and say, "You know, so and so said the same thing you have been telling me." He picks my ego up from the floor, where it had fallen following the first student's report. The truth, however, is that the first student did learn something that I had not properly communicated to him when I "taught" it to him originally.

Communication at least with players and teachers of all stringed instruments is essential to our development of broad concepts of musical understanding and performance, but we must also expose ourselves to as many "successful" concepts of performance on the double bass as we possibly can. The realization that no one knows it all should make us reach out, so that we never stop growing (which is learning, is it not?). The most important musical word I know is *humility*. It is the word that keeps teachers from getting stuck with tradition and makes them seek concepts that are based on intellectual comprehension and the science of pedagogy and performance. It is the word that fosters communication and matures an artist's performance. It is the word that was so beautifully expressed by Arturo Toscanini, when he was in his seventies. At a rehearsal during the time when I was with the N.B.C. Symphony he said, "You remember when we did this symphony three years ago? It was not right. The tempo was wrong, the balance was not right in the second movement. . . ." He added several other criticisms, all of *his* interpretation. Then he concluded with, "But now I am three years older and now know better."

Toscanini's well never ran dry. He made a continuing effort to find the composer's intent. We have all known conductors and soloists whose wells have "run dry," in many cases because they unconsciously stopped the search along the way, believing they had already found the composer's true meaning and intent. Others have imposed interpretations on the music that were never intended by the composer because they "knew better" how the work should have been written. Some have stopped the search and have contrived a means of establishing their own identity in the music, losing interest in the music itself, and in the process also losing humility.

Of course, we can question minute aspects of the scores of almost every composer, no matter how great his genius. Among the hundreds of thousands of notes required to produce the literary output of a Haydn or a Beethoven there is bound to be an erroneous stroke of the pen or an unclear notation. There are certainly places to be questioned, but only in the search for intent, not to create our own vision of what "it should have been." To this day, I am not certain why Beethoven wrote grace notes for the basses in the beginning of the *Marche Funèbre* of the Third Symphony and then wrote out similar figures as regular notes several bars later. I think I know why, but I am not perfectly sure, and I will always wish I *really* knew.

Similarly there is a place in the first movement of the Seventh Symphony where Beethoven marked the last eighth note of the measure piano, leaving the preceding sixteenth forte. It is impossible to have an entire section play this passage piano, yet the theme itself starts with the sixteenth note of the same dotted eighth, sixteenth, eighth rhythm. It would seem that the *p* was carelessly written and seems to occur under the last eighth rather than under the sixteenth note preceding it, where musically it would coincide with the thematic statement and technically it would be playable by all. It is this sort of search for the composer's intent in which we all must involve ourselves, not in order to put a different face on a composition because "That's the way I like it," or because we are bored with the work and are looking for a new dimension, one not intended by the composer. This latter attitude creates our own "spectacular," for our *own intent,* and is the first big step toward losing humility. I have heard great technical artistry but no great musical messages from a performer, conductor, or student who gives in to egotistical musical fantasy at the cost of humility. Although humility does not insure our finding the truth, it will at least insure an honest search for it.

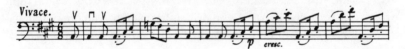

SOUND PRODUCTION

In view of the influences that shaped many of my attitudes toward teaching and performance, it is only logical that I seek a sound compatible with the string family. When I am playing chamber music, in which the doubling of the cello is so prevalent, I will "shadow" the sound of the cellist. For me there is no greater compliment than to have an educated listener comment, "The sounds of the cello and bass were balanced to the point where I could not separate them when they played the same line." I consider this as mostly my achievement, because I know I am doing my best to accomplish this balance. The cellist reaches out in many ways to achieve uniformity but does not try to match the sound concept of the bassist. The cello has one of the most beautiful voices in solo and ensemble literature; thus it is vanity to expect a cellist to change his tonal colors to blend with the bass. So it is my responsibility to find a way of blending and bending without losing the depth and personality of the double bass. I simply think of it as the deepest sounding instrument in the string family. It then becomes an extension of the cello, just as the cello is an extension of the upper strings in building the complete range of pitch, tone colors, and sonorities peculiar to the string family.

As a member of the Baroque Chamber Players, I played the only stringed instrument in consort with harpsichord, flute, and oboe. Here my role was more that of the cellist, since to have the continuo line, and sometimes solo lines, sound in the register written, it is naturally necessary for the double bass to play an octave higher. Finally, like most bassists, I have also played solo works with orchestra, and that experience has made me aware of the problems in yet another phase of performance.

All these involvements have only strengthened my long-held conviction that the bass is an integral member of the string family both pedagogically and musically. Our sound must be produced according to the same principles all the other bowed strings use, and it must blend with any of them. The means we use for bow articulation must also be based on the same principles used by the other strings. Of course there will be adjustments and modifications necessitated by the greater length and thickness of our strings. Their resultant resistance is proportionately much greater than the difference in weight between a bass bow and those of the upper strings. Most bass bows weigh barely twice as much as a violin bow, but if their weights were in the same proportion to the resistances they deal with, the bass bows would be clubs, unyielding, too heavy to handle and best used in battle, not in the performance of music.

Our efforts and training must parallel almost every aspect of string playing in general. We must know how to start a sound or tone with or without an attack; play with a slow or a fast bow; at the bridge or near the fingerboard and everywhere in between; off the string and on the string and all gradations in between. I am concerned about polarization of approaches to the use of the bow, caused by exaggeration of certain practices advanced by teachers of the double bass and/or misunderstandings on the part of students. I have in mind the excessive concentration on the ''slow bow,'' the ''fast bow,'' playing primarily at the bridge, avoiding playing near the bridge, starting every note with an attack, achieving attacks only with the rush of bow hair over the strings without sufficient pressure at the beginning of the stroke. Most of these techniques are part of the total usage of the bow. One needs experience with and control of all types of bowing in order to have a full range of colors and textures. A truly great artist on the bass (or any other stringed instrument) must include all concepts in his performance. Many talented bassists display only a partial spectrum of musical expression because their training and/or thinking has limited their exploration of the traditional bowing techniques. That is a luxury we cannot afford on the double bass. In view of the control we need to parallel the expressiveness of the cello or the violin, we need every color and texture available, plus *subtle* exaggeration to get similar results.

Our results must be compatible with the sound of the other strings, not extraordinary to the ear. The *greatly* exaggerated paths we sometimes take to make up for our inability to perform as other string players do constitute evasions of our responsibilities to sound or misconceptions of our potential. If one were to start a scale in the violins and descend gradually into the register of the double bass, via the violas and the cellos, it should not be apparent when each section stops and the next lower one begins. This should hold for all types of bowings—legato, staccato, spiccato, etc.—and for all textures and nuances.

In the end, sound is energy. This energy is created by the pressure, speed, and resistance we use in producing sounds with the bow. It emanates from the body as we draw the bow, maneuver the bass, and work the left arm and hand. If you look at a performer carefully, you can see the subtle play of these forces, and even if you cannot hear the notes you can almost imagine the kind of sound that is being produced. Imagine an explosion: the greatest energy is released in the first stage; afterward things set in motion by the initial burst of energy diminish in their thrust. To visualize an explosion is also to visualize a violent attack with the bow, after which there is a sustaining of a forte. The first inch or two of bow exerts great speed and pressure, but then speed is replaced by pressure and resistance to maintain the forte. To leave out any aspect of the three forces is to leave out some of the energy required to give an attack its proper character. At a point in a phrase where the intensity increases, perhaps for a climactic effect, the energy level also increases. Conversely, in achieving placidity in a phrase, the energy level is low. Thinking this way should allow one to see the correlations between the use of pressure, speed, and resistance and the levels of energy required in the different functions the bow has to fulfil.

Loudness is not always commensurate with depth of sound. Nor is clarity commensurate with forte or piano; it can be part of either. Excess resistance does not provide the fullest sound if the bow speed is severely restricted. In the first long E in the recitative of Beethoven's Ninth Symphony, after the articulation (attack) of the E, speed decreases almost immediately and gives way to resistance in order to sustain the note for four beats. However, the substitution or realignment must still result in a dramatic and moving texture, not in a static character.

One can do many things in writing, but unfortunately one cannot adequately describe sound without actually producing it. I can only say what is uppermost in my mind in the production of sound. I seek the deep sonority or fundamental of each tone I produce, for I play *the bass* of the string ensemble. I seek in each sound a resonance so that there is a sense of the instrument, not just the string, vibrating under the bow. I usually seek a string reaction that provides resistance to the bow, so that I can feel the bow sinking into that "ledge of resistance" under the hair and on the "bridge side" of the hair. Once that "ledge of resistance" is realized for almost any volume, the bow will not skim over the string but will find control through resistance in sync with the speed and pressure being used. I also seek the feeling that I am projecting. Finally, I seek the color in ensemble that will be an extension of the prevailing sonorities being produced by the rest of the strings. Even if they are wrong, I must match them, for if I do not, no matter how right I am in my personal concept, I will neither enhance the community sound nor project a meaningful quality to the ensemble or to the audience. My refusing to conform to the ensemble will not correct anything, and if I am not flexible enough to adapt and blend with the others I will not learn anything.

Posture

Performance involves athletic activity. Behavior in performance demands that we achieve balance for that physical activity. When playing an instrument the size of the double bass, which is too large for most humans to deal with, it is essential that we make the best use of the body. We face the unnatural situation of the right arm and the right side of the body reaching down while the left arm functions on a higher plane. This configuration alone is enough to take its toll on our skeletal-muscular structure over the years, without our getting into other, unnecessary positions of imbalance.

Instinctively as well as through training, a fine athlete will support every motion by a balanced position of the body. There is a proper pedestal (position of legs–feet) that supports every gesture from the thighs on up. In tennis, Ping-Pong, batting a baseball, all aspects of football, or any sport where both sides of the body are involved, we can assume a position that will support the various movements of the upper body. In playing the bass, the ever-shifting torso, resulting from the execution of a full bow stroke and the ever-shifting left arm, requires constant adjustment of the supporting mechanism. That does not mean ever-shifting legs, but it does mean one should anticipate the need to rebalance and choose a stance from which one can do so as quickly as possible and as often as necessary. The moving upper torso is rebalancing even when the stance seems to remain intact. One may also be unconsciously shifting the weight from one leg to the other.

I see a boxer in his position of readiness assuming the pedestal and balance similar to that needed for playing in thumb position. When we visualize the stances necessary for balance we might liken the act of pulling a chest expander apart to drawing a down-bow to the tip, and the feat of compressing a large coil spring to returning a full up-bow to the frog. Rebalancing is always taking place somewhere in the body, and the pedestal must be able to support all these motions without putting strain on the lower back. The feet must be placed so they support the torso, wherever it is going, with the head leading. But if the head extends beyond the pedestal, the lower back will have to bear the brunt of the support. With few exceptions, an athlete whose head goes beyond his pedestal and whose legs are together and straight is an athlete in trouble.

When the bass is played in the seated position, part of the pedestal is the stool. Even then the placement of the legs–feet is crucial, and it is essential that the entire pelvis be supported by the stool. It is not necessary to sit well back on the stool, just make sure that both buttocks rest on it. If only one rests on the stool, the unsupported side will tend to drop, while the supported side will be pushed up, causing an imbalance that may affect the spine. Sitting often causes other problems. In trying to achieve better access to thumb position, one tends to ignore the needs of the bow arm and to place the bass more in front of the body, instead of keeping it along the left thigh with the back corner of the bass into the left side of the crotch. This forces the bow arm to reach out much farther for the G-string, and in the process the torso is twisted. As the G-string is so predominant in solo playing, if this behavior becomes a habit, in time it will be damaging to the back.

Every instrument has its occupational hazards. The bass is such a large instrument it is best played by one well over six feet tall. For the violinist the problem is not the size of the instrument but that the left arm is constantly up in the air. For the flutist it is that both arms always go toward the right side of the body. In all these cases, as with the double bass, we should make the best use of the body through proper positioning and balance, much as athletes do.

Naturally each instrument has its own personality and textural possibilities. That is what makes each stringed instrument fascinating for the performer and the composer. The subtle use of different textures and articulations makes possible unique tonal and expressive characteristics not only for each member of the string family but for every individual who has learned how to express through his or her instrument what is in the "mind's ear." For me it has always been a thrill to be a member of that most versatile family of instruments, in which my involvement is a constant challenge and reward.

Despite all that we have already learned about the problems of playing the double bass, there is still much to explore. We must not accept blindly the teachings of our double bass ancestors, but we must know why we are doing what we are doing—physically, musically, and intellectually. Tradition has not misled us so much as it has not provided all the answers. We must accept what has been passed on to us until we understand enough to confirm or deny its validity. Unfortunately, no one of us knows all the answers, and total comprehension lies farther up the road than we can reach in the time life allots us. Thus, as in all things, it remains the challenge for those who follow to continue the quest.

Franco Gulli

Translated from the Italian by Linda Nemerow

Evolution of Violin Technique in Relation to Interpretive Problems of Our Time

When the spiritual content of a musical work is immutable, the way of interpreting and executing it has a continuous evolution over time. In order to comprehend this idea, one might compare the first recordings made by famous artists with performances on more recent recordings. It is even more interesting to listen to the same work as recorded by a violinist early in his career and in a subsequent version performed by him at a later age. Usually one perceives quite a different execution of the text, not only from a musical standpoint, but with respect to musical detail: the audible shifts that characterized violin performances for years and many of the expressive slides, used indiscriminately and immoderately in earlier times, have disappeared.

In the last thirty years, the public's auditory perception has been greatly refined as a direct result of the appearance of long-playing records (and, later, tapes and cassettes) and the enormous dissemination of classical music by an extensive recording industry. Dubious intonation and unpleasant sounds are no longer acceptable.

In order to achieve a more precise and objective execution, technical knowledge must be continuously renewed by developing the capacity of the four fingers of the left hand and adapting the bow technique to meet the sonic requirements of ever-larger concert halls.

Fifty years ago, Carl Flesch began to chart new and unexplored pathways in his fundamental work, *The Art of Violin Playing*. The extraordinary result of his lifelong research is contained in an equally important volume, *The Art of Fingering for the Violinist*, which appeared posthumously. Despite the widespread dissemination of the works of Flesch and other authors who are careful not to

succumb to the convenient praises of an interpretation overbur-
dened with years of tradition, few violinists take an interest in the
need for a constant evolution of instrumental technique. I have dis-
covered during my long experience in instructing students of different levels, that they prefer an erroneous, accepted solution to one
that is suited to the correct musical performance of a passage requir-
ing instrumental perfection. These notes are directed particularly to
these maturing students.

The position of the body and of the arms and the angle of the left
hand to the fingerboard are very important. When I ask a student to
lean on both feet, to relax completely, and then to lift his left arm
naturally, he will usually finish the upward motion with his body
shifted toward the left and the left hand at mouth level or slightly
higher. This should, therefore, be the left-arm position throughout
the performance, instead of the forced and, unfortunately, common
position toward the center of the body with the elbow close to the
stomach.

Distinct benefits may be gained from shifting with correct posture,
namely, the ability to rotate the arm with ease toward the right and
so keep the hand from touching the body of the instrument and
thereby actuate a single, smooth movement. Problems of clarity and
intonation are eased once we eliminate the need for further adjustments to get us past the fourth or fifth position.

The angle of the left hand to the fingerboard is extremely important, for, in my opinion, it should be the same on any string and in
any position. In order to understand what I mean by a constant
angle, try to play the excerpts in Exx. 1, 2, and 3 with the fingerings
given. The upper fingerings are the ones I recommend.

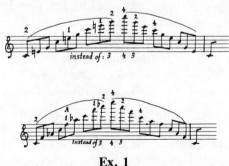

Ex. 1

Ex. 2. Paganini, Concerto in D major, first movement.

Ex. 3. Ernst, Concerto in F♯ minor.

The position of the thumb cannot be determined precisely since the shape of the hand varies from person to person. Let us start with the principle that the instrument is held by the pressure of the chin and not by the hand. The thumb, therefore, should be placed in such a way that the fingers are ready to play without having to make a long crossing before meeting the string. When the thumb is held back, slightly behind the first finger, it permits a constant angle with the fingerboard, both in the lower positions and when overcoming the obstacle posed by the instrument itself in reaching for higher position. The base of the index finger thus lightly touches the neck of the violin without pressure, greatly facilitating shifts, and preventing stiffness during the execution of long, rapid works like a *perpetuum mobile*. Keeping the fingertips close to the strings also helps to prevent the annoying noises made when the fingers hit the strings percussively from above, sounds that become intolerable on recordings or broadcasts.

The use of new fingerings is undoubtedly the most distinctive feature in the development of left-hand technique. Incredible as it may seem, the even positions are still rejected in favor of longer shifts, which make the intonation less certain, despite the fact that it is obviously easier to shift to a neighboring position than to a more distant one. In Ex. 4 the upper fingering is certainly preferable to the lower, traditional one, which is recommended in almost all editions. Fingerings that respect phrasing, prevent erroneous accents, and foster sonic equality are even more important, as in Exx. 5-9.

Ex. 4.   Mozart, Concerto in D major, K.218, first movement.

Ex. 5.   Bach, Gavotte from Partita in E major.

Ex. 6.   Bach, Allemande from Partita in D minor.

Ex. 7.   Schubert, Sonata in A minor, D.385, second movement.

Ex. 8.   Beethoven, Sonata Op. 30, No. 2, first movement.

Ex. 9.   Brahms, Sonata in G major, second
movement.

Greater use of stretches and fingered octaves (which are the direct
result of the stretches) is advisable in order to minimize audible
shifts and unnecessary slides in Ex. 10. It is evident in Ex. 11 that
the use of fingered octaves keeps a descending shift from being
followed immediately by an ascending one, thus facilitating correct
musical phrasing and preventing an incorrect accent on the first G''''
that is virtually unavoidable with the conventional 1–4, 1–4 fingering. Two shifts are similarly avoided in Exx. 12 and 13.

Ex. 10.   Beethoven, Concerto Op. 61, first
movement.

Ex. 11.   Beethoven, Concerto Op. 61, first
movement.

Ex. 12.   Wieniawski, Scherzo Tarantelle.

Ex. 13. Mendelssohn, Concerto Op. 64, first movement.

In Ex. 14 a combination of fingered octaves and octaves performed with an unchanging 1–3 fingering throughout the chromatic ascent avoids making two descending shifts.

Ex. 14. Wieniawski, Concerto No. 2, first movement.

Every violinist knows the difficulty of playing the passage in Ex. 15 with perfect intonation and without accents caused by wide left-arm movements.

Ex. 15. Brahms, Concerto Op. 77, first movement.

The shifts are shorter and the hand does not even change its angle with 3–1, 4–2 fingering in the fourth measure.

I feel that it is virtually impossible to discard fingered octaves in Ex. 16. In order to avoid a long sequence of slides using traditional fingerings, one ordinarily resorts to portando bowing, which destroys the serenity of this light counterpoint to the theme in the oboe. This problem is solved by employing fingered octaves, shifting on semitones, and making bow changes between whole-tones.

Ex. 16. Brahms, Concerto Op. 77, second movement.

Ex. 17. Brahms, Concerto Op. 77, first movement.

There are certain cases in which a stretch exceeds the reach of the fourth finger on a normal-sized hand. In order to avoid shifting that could make the intonation dubious, one should be well aware of the base position from which the stretch is most easily made. In Ex. 17, the tenth D♯–F♯ is virtually impossible to execute without moving the hand slightly when the base position of the preceding E–C♯ is the third, but is aided quite surprisingly when the E–C♯ is played in fourth position. The value of this unconventional fingering lies also in the natural ability of the second and third fingers to make the link to the next F♯–D♯ double-stop.

Ex. 18. Prokofiev, Concerto Op. 19, first movement.

The use of stretches can make the execution of quick movements clearer than would be possible with continuous string-crossings. It also has the important musical advantage of allowing one to play groups of slurred notes, as in Ex. 18, on the same string and with the same sound quality. Exx. 19 and 20 are two more instances showing the value of stretches in place of a shift.

Ex. 19.   Debussy, Sonata, second movement.

Ex. 20.   Paganini, Concerto No. 2, third movement.

Often a combination of stretches *followed* by a shift improves the speed and clarity of the execution, as in Ex. 21, where the first C is played with a stretch of the second finger and *then* the hand moves to second position. In Ex. 22, the second measure is played in second position, the F by means of a backward stretch, after which the hand returns to first position.

Ex. 21.   Paganini, Capriccio No. 5.

Ex. 22.   Beethoven, Sonata Op. 30, No. 3, third movement.

In Ex. 23 a shift from first to second position at the beginning of the second measure and a stretch to the D''' prevent a slide that would not only interrupt the character of the variation but also cause a false accent on the third 32nd note of the second measure.

46   *Franco Gulli*

Ex. 23.   Beethoven, Sonata Op. 12, No. 1, second movement.

The choice of the proper string and, consequently, of the correct fingering are crucial to the performance of a work that requires great color and variety of accent, like a Beethoven sonata. Ex. 24 demonstrates a musically logical fingering typical of Flesch's and Szigeti's interesting fingerings. In the third to the last measure the sforzando applies only to the first F♯. Therefore I suggest using the G-string on the first note and then passing to second position on the D-string, thus acquiring an essential tonal difference.

Ex. 24.   Beethoven, Sonata Op. 30, No. 3, third movement.

In Ex. 25 we have two sforzandi in the second measure and a decrescendo in the third. I propose that the stronger G-string should

Ex. 25.   Beethoven, Sonata Op. 24, first movement.

be used to play the sforzandi, and the gentler D-string for the following measure without the sforzandi, and for the decrescendo.

While the practice of scales and arpeggios always provides excellent exercise for finger agility, shifts, and intonation, it should be noted that traditional fingerings are not always applicable to the execution of a work in which scales and arpeggios must be played very rapidly. In these cases it is better to space the shifts farther apart, as in Exx. 26 and 27.

Ex. 26

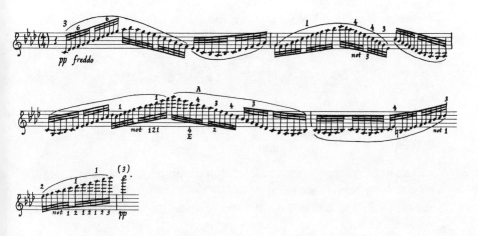

Ex. 27.   Prokofiev, Sonata Op. 80, first movement and finale.

The little scale so highly feared in the Scherzo of Prokofiev's Concerto Op. 19, in which the minimum metronome marking is $\downarrow$ = 160, is virtually unexecutable with conventional fingering. Three solutions are suggested in Ex. 28. Joseph Szigeti suggests starting in seventh position so there is but one shift between the G'''' and the A''''. However, the great difficulty of placing the first finger on the A''' makes this fingering risky. David Oistrakh begins in third position and uses the finger sequence 123, 1234, 1234, playing the scale entirely on the E-string. The upper fingering is almost identical to Oistrakh's, but it offers a tiny bit more time at the beginning, which, perhaps, is useful after the jump of position between D'''' and A'''. After much consideration, I have finally decided to adopt this last solution.

Ex. 28. Prokofiev, Concerto Op. 19, second movement.

It is sometimes useful to reduce the number of shifts where great evenness is required. With my fingering, there are only two shifts in Ex. 29 instead of the three prescribed by conventional fingerings.

Ex. 29. Beethoven, Concerto Op. 61, first movement.

The shift where the rhythmic configuration permits slightly more time is a fundamental rule to be applied to particularly difficult passages, as in Ex. 30. In Ex. 31, according to the old fingering, between the chords on either side of the asterisk, the first finger, which is used for the A''' of the C–E–A chord, must move extremely fast in order to reach the G♯'' of the following G♯–E–D chord. There is a bit more time in the upper fingering.

Ex. 30. Viotti, Concerto No. 22, third movement.

Ex. 31. Brahms, Concerto Op. 77, first movement.

A double-stop of an augmented fourth always presents an intonation problem, especially for violinists with thicker than average fingers. It is perfectly useless to spend hours of practice trying to force the second finger *under* the third in Exx. 32 and 33. The C♯ will always be flat. The problem is solved magically by first preparing the second finger, and *then* placing the third over it. We encounter the same problem in Exx. 34 and 35.

Ex. 32.   Bach, Fugue from Sonata in G minor.

Ex. 33.   Bach, Courant from Partita in D minor.

Ex. 34.   Prokofiev, Sonata Op. 80, second
            movement.

Ex. 35.   Paganini, Capriccio No. 15.

The correct movement of the voices in polyphonic pieces is extremely important. (I won't even mention Bach's Sonatas and Partitas for Solo Violin since that discussion would lead us astray.) One

of the most problematic musical and technical passages in our literature occurs at the beginning of Beethoven's "Kreutzer" Sonata.
Flesch suggests an interesting fingering that has inspired me to find
another way to play the opening measures, shown in Ex. 36, so that
the voices will remain independent and thereby give the phrase new
instrumental color after the forte of the opening chord. (This phrase,
incidentally, is similar to the opening of the Seventh Symphony, also
written in A major.) As risky as the 2–4 fingering on the E'–E''
octave initially seems, the violinist acquainted with fingered octaves
will undoubtedly prefer it because the shift is shortened, and the
second and fourth fingers are not involved in playing the preceding
G♯–B double-stop.

Ex. 36.   Beethoven, Sonata Op. 47, first move-
              ment.

In 1903 Friedrich Steinhausen maintained in his important
treatise, *Physiology of the Bow Arm,* that bowing power and action
reside in the arm and forearm, while the wrist and the fingers *follow*
the movement of the arm. Today I notice that many young people
still give great priority to wrist and finger movement, especially
when playing détaché and spiccato. They keep the rest of the arm
almost inactive, resulting in a continual change in the point of contact between the bow hair and the string, which creates an irregular-
ity in tonal output. When we acknowledge the fact that in order for
the string to vibrate regularly the bow must be at right angles to it, it
follows that up- and down-bow movements remain the same
whether all the bow is used or only a small part of it, as in the case of
fast détaché or spiccato. In some special instances a slightly oblique
bowing will produce a singular tonal effect, but those cases are the
exception, not the rule.

Much has been written and taught on the method of holding the
bow. The following is a theoretical view: If the thumb and the middle
finger form a ring to hold the stick, the other fingers must move

slightly apart in order to control more of the surface of the stick. In this way it is easier to use the weight of the whole arm from the shoulder to produce an even tone at the frog as well as at the tip. The shoulder must not be raised, since the wrist and the fingers would then be forced to exert pressure on the bow stick, thereby stiffening the muscles and precluding any possibility of producing brilliant bowings. While it is not my purpose to establish a rule, I see the upper arm held parallel to the bow stick as the proper right-arm posture. The arm and forearm are, therefore, slightly higher when playing on the G-string and lower on the E. This adjustment is easily made when standing in front of a mirror with the bow at the midpoint on the strings.

Insufficient understanding of right-arm movement is apparent in the notion that a fortissimo can be achieved by mere bow pressure on the strings. While this is partly true, it should be remembered that the bow speed may be used to produce a tone that is clear and not scratchy. The accelerative and decelerative speed of the bow are also very important when playing a final note pianissimo in the extreme upper register. These notes are often imperceptible in their final phases because the bow speed is not completely regular. To remedy that fault, I recognize that the bow is heaviest at the frog, and that its weight diminishes progressively toward the tip. Therefore I begin the note at the frog with a very slow, flowing movement, since the string vibrates by the weight of the bow, and I speed up as I approach the tip to compensate for the progressive weight loss. This problem is further resolved by slightly rotating the stick toward the bridge so as to allow all of the hair to touch the string.

By distribution of the bow I also mean the amount of bow to be used on a sequence of notes of unequal duration, as for example in the Siciliana rhythm ♪.♫♩, where we find the equivalent of three sixteenth notes during the first note, followed by one sixteenth, and it, in turn, is followed by the equivalent of two sixteenths. If we play the second of these notes with the same amount of bow used for the first, we create an accent that totally spoils the musical flow. It is precisely for this reason that the violinist must divide the bow length according to the duration of the note, thus varying the placement of the bow on the string. The execution of this rhythm in the following manner ♪.♫♩ is preferable to ♪.♫♩, and is quite common today.

While I have rarely encountered problems working with fairly gifted students on the down-bow motion, I have very often detected what I consider an entirely erroneous up-bow movement. Many young violinists raise the wrist and turn the fingers toward the right almost halfway between the tip and the frog. As a result, half the bow is *pushed* and the rest is *pulled* toward the frog. The motion of the bow is certainly not consistent, since after half the bow is used the bow hair forms an acute angle instead of a right angle with the string, which does not allow the string to vibrate evenly.

The solution to the problem is easier than it would seem. The arm, from the shoulder to the knuckles, must form a smooth curve, with the upper arm, the forearm, and the hand all on the same plane. In this way all bowings, from a sequence of long notes to a fast spic-cato, from a four-note chord to a staccato, are played with a horizontal arm motion, allowing the string to "breathe."

Moreover, the change from up- to down-bow at the frog must be played with a motion of the entire arm, while the wrist and fingers are never rigid, but follow the movement of the arm without *actively* participating in the change of bow.

Do not forget the premise that the bow touches the string while the violin remains immobile is basic to correct bowing technique. If one moves the violin so that the strings meet the bow, as many players do, one must constantly adjust the movement of the bow during and after the string-crossings (like Paganini's Second Capriccio). An unfortunate unevenness in rhythm and sonority will result.

Although great importance is attached to bowing in violin technique, the legato, which is extremely valuable in the execution of lengthy phrases, has received little attention. (Kreutzer's Etude No. 1 is among the few exceptions.) Recently there has been an increasing tendency to play portando a phrase that requires great interpretive serenity. Students are sometimes taught to ease the bow pressure between tied notes. I do not agree with this for two reasons. First, when the composer gives no sign that a portando is required, the performer is bound to respect his intention. Second, and perhaps more significant, a portando bowing could confer equal tension to every note, in contradiction to the laws of diatonic and chromatic harmony. It would not be suitable to perform the measures following the cadenza in the first movement of the Beethoven

concerto in the manner indicated by the markings in Ex. 37. I would
insist instead on the correct distribution of bow speed for natural
phrasing, with light tension on the first two measures and relaxation
on the third and fourth. Moreover, I do not think it possible to divide
the bowings more than the passage in Ex. 38 suggests.

Ex. 37.   Beethoven, Concerto Op. 61, first
movement.

Ex. 38.   Beethoven, Sonata Op. 12, No. 3, second movement.

What I call bow distribution is sometimes quite problematic, as in
Ex. 39, because of the alternation of slurs and brief, separated notes.
It is, therefore, best to play the fifth eighth note of each measure
with the same bow direction as was used for the first four.

Ex. 39.   Bach, Gavotte from Partita in E major.

We often encounter long sequences of separated notes suddenly
followed by groups of tied notes, particularly in fast movements of
Baroque music. The separate notes are played with the upper part of
the bow. Much more bow is needed for the sets of three tied notes in
Ex. 40 than for a single note. (Theoretically, the amount of bow
needed for the three tied notes is three times as much.) In order to
prevent a stong accent on the last of the separate notes and yet reach

the part of the bow where the three tied notes can best be played, we should descend *progressively,* during the first measure of the example, from the upper to the middle part of the bow, and use more than just the note preceding the tie for this displacement. I suggest practicing this bowing, which I consider very important, during daily scale work, starting at the point with groups of repeated notes, descending toward the frog, sustaining the same sonority and rhythmic regularity, and then returning to the point. Ex. 41, an example of original Bach phrasing, is particularly interesting. Knowledge of the point of departure of each bowing is extremely important in order to play the combination of separate notes, the short tie, and the long ties. Practice this only after you have established correct bowing distribution, otherwise you will be wasting your time.

Ex. 40.   Bach, Gigue from Partita in D minor.

Ex. 41.   Bach, Presto from Sonata in G minor.
             U.B. =upper part of bow
             W.B. =whole bow
             L.B. =lower part of bow

Often an otherwise musically gifted student forgets to observe the starting and ending points of a theme or an incidental theme. Incorrect phrasing can result from improper bowing, especially when the rhythmic pulse is an important part of the musical context. By using the upper bowing in Ex. 42 one can avoid an accent on the B♭ quarter note of the second bar. Such an accent would impede the flow of the phrase. Similar situations occur in Exx. 43 and 44. When we encounter a sequence of accents or sforzandi inscribed by the composer, bowings that permit even execution of dynamic signs are preferable, as in Ex. 45.

Ex. 42. Beethoven, Sonata Op. 30, No. 2, first movement.

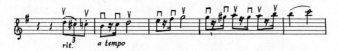

Ex. 43. Handel, Sonata in D major, third movement.

Ex. 44. Beethoven, Sonata Op. 96, first movement.

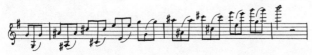

Ex. 45. Beethoven, Sonata Op. 30, No. 3, first movement.

Many violinists have difficulty with passages like the one given in Ex. 46, where it seems appropriate to devote more bow to the two slurred notes than to the separate ones. This technique almost always results in double-stops instead of broken octaves. Greater articulation is achieved when more force is applied to the up-bow on the first note of each triplet and the two tied notes are played with a simple reflex motion.

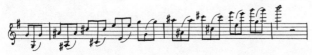

Ex. 46. Mendelssohn, Concerto Op. 64, first movement.

Ex. 47. Viotti, Concerto No. 22, third movement.

In Ex. 47 the active movement is concentrated on the shorter
down-bow at the tip, rather than on the longer note, which is played
with a reflex bowing.

The staccato is a type of bowing derived from the need to play the
martelé at a fast tempo. The staccato has since become an almost
exclusively virtuoso type of bowing, especially admired by colleagues and students who have difficulty playing it. In a concert hall,
the so-called flying staccato is rarely perceptible, particularly in its
initial phases. There are, however, moments in violin literature
when this bowing must be considered in order to do justice to the
composer's intention. Many violinists naturally possess a brilliant
staccato that is attainable almost always at an immutable metronomic speed. In Exx. 48, 49, and 50, however, the staccato must
be played in the precise tempo of the musical context and with very
consistent sonority.

Ex. 48. Paganini, Concerto in D major, third
movement.

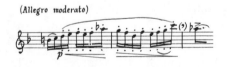

Ex. 49. Wieniawski, Concerto No. 2, third
movement.

Ex. 50. Prokofiev, Concerto Op. 19, first movement.

In Ex. 48, the metronomic speed is approximately ♩ = 126. It is slightly faster in Ex. 49, but ♩ = 96 in Ex. 50. Great mastery and absolute control of the staccato's speed are therefore indispensable. Practicing this bowing can be facilitated by knowing that even in these cases the string must vibrate evenly (that is, with a right angle between the bow hair and the string). The movement is similar to that of the détaché, but instead of playing the sequence of notes alternately up and down, one proceeds in the same bowing direction, retaining the impulse in the arm and forearm, while the wrist and fingers follow without actively participating. Vertical movements between notes are not advisable; instead, the separation is made by simply arresting the flow of the bow.

I hope that these remarks and musical illustrations will be of value to those young people for whom playing the violin represents not merely a job but continual research. I am firmly convinced that in a few years many of my ideas and suggestions will be superseded, and I hope to be among those who have found new solutions.

I would like to close with a thought by Ferruccio Busoni:

> When a work is finished, we have accomplished such progress that the work is already surpassed, endowing its authorship with the capacity for continual development. This fosters the beginning of a new work and the process goes on forever (as can be seen in Michelangelo, Goethe, Verdi) without ever having said all.

Georges Janzer

Reflections on Tempo Indications

In spite of having concertized around the world with the Vegh Quartet for 37 years, I have always enjoyed playing chamber music in private life, just for the pleasure of making music (*Hausmusik*), often playing with amateur musicians.

On one of these occasions, during a string sextet, the second violinist suddenly played a phrase distinctly slower, a phrase that was important melodically. The first violinist stopped and asked him the reason for his change in tempo.

"It is marked '*Tranquillo*' at that place in my part so it has to be played slower," answered the second violinist.

"But *tranquillo* means 'quiet,' not 'slow,'" said the first violinist. "It is an expression, not a tempo indication."

Then we played that passage again, not slower, but just with a quiet expression—and it was beautiful.

I mention this episode because this little exchange settled in my brain and later gave me the impulse to examine all the tempo indications that I had learned and that are generally taken for granted around the world. Where did they originate, *what is their real meaning?* And why do we use Italian words for almost all tempo indications? For the answer we have to go back quite far in history.

Except for the early medieval songs of the troubadours, which were in great part improvised and not written down, we cannot deny that occidental music originates from Italy, and therefore the tempo markings are in Italian. But why just Italian? Why did the whole civilized world adopt the Italian markings? I think it must have been the great power, political as well as cultural, of the Catholic Church. It had tremendous influence in earlier centuries and very cleverly used everything it could to reinforce and increase that influence. The

58

Gregorian chants were written down so they could be spread over the entire Christian world.

Then came such composers as Palestrina, Orlando di Lasso, Monteverdi, Vivaldi, Pergolese, Tartini, and hundreds of others, whose works are still on concert programs around the world. Being Italians, they naturally used their own language to mark their pieces. These composers were so important, distinguished, and numerous in their time, and had such a great influence on the whole musical world, that composers of other nationalities, like Gluck, Bach, Handel, and Purcell, also adopted their indications and markings, and so Italian became the "official" musical language.

So far, so good. But, although these musicians and their German, English, etc., contemporaries knew the exact meaning of the words they were using, the real meanings of many of them were slightly altered through the centuries.

When I began to play violin, I was six years old and spoke only Hungarian. So in studying music I had to learn that *Adagio* means "slow" and *Presto* means "fast." I thought at that time that these funny words were technical terms, invented especially to indicate different tempi in music. I knew they were Italian, but I was very surprised when I later learned that they were just common Italian words, still used today in conversation. Unfortunately in my early years of study I learned that *tranquillo* means "slower than the mean tempo" and that *con anima* means "faster." And of course that is *not* true.

The Baroque composers used very few terms for their tempo indications: *Lento, Adagio, Largo, Andante, Allegro, Vivace, Presto*. Although all these words were taken from the Italian language of that period, they had the same meanings as the dictionary gives today. And this point is important! With the passage of time we attributed slightly different meanings to many of them. For example, *Lento* and *Adagio* both mean "slow," but *Largo* means "large, broad" and not specifically slow. *Largo* is more of a character than a tempo indication. We can play a relatively flowing piece "large" or "broad." An *Andante* movement can be played "large" if the melodic line requires it, or in the same *Andante* we can play some quiet sixteenth-note passages "broad."

It is similar with fast movements: *Presto* means "fast" in Italian, but *Vivace* is "lively, with life," and *Allegro* means "joyful, in a good mood." When we see an *Allegro* indication we tend to assume that the movement is fast. But not necessarily! Certainly it is not a slow movement, but we have to distinguish and take the original meaning of the word. This misunderstanding explains why we so often hear Baroque *Allegro* movements played so fast—too fast.

Going on in the history of music, we arrive at the classical composers. During the time of Haydn and Mozart we rarely find more complicated or more detailed indications than were used in the Baroque (many of their oeuvres—quartets, symphonies—have the simple indications for the four movements: *Allegro, Adagio, Allegretto, Allegro*), but Beethoven felt the need of giving more precise and more detailed indications to express his music. Naturally, all his contemporaries and the following generations of composers followed suit. Thus were born indications like *Andante un poco allegretto, Allegro ma non troppo, Adagio molto espressivo, Allegretto scherzando*. Those indications, too, should be understood in light of their literal translations or true meanings.

Other kinds of indications came into being also. These were not indications for the whole movement (which would be indicated at the beginning of the piece), but were related to a specific part of it or pertained to a particular phrase, such as *tranquillo, largamente, con anima, agitato*. These are *not* tempo indications, although they are usually considered as such today. I would call them "character indications," and I refer again to the original meanings of the words. When a particular phrase of an *Allegro* movement is marked *tranquillo,* it should be played "quietly" but not necessarily "more slowly." Naturally, we cannot rush when we have to play quietly, but to make that phrase slower purposely is erroneous. A lot depends on the phrase in question, and on the melodic line, which sometimes requires a slightly slower tempo. But it is not a rule that we *automatically* slow down when a passage is marked *tranquillo*. With this consideration in mind, we will find that many places marked *tranquillo* can be played very beautifully and with quiet expression without affecting the tempo. Remember, when a composer wants a phrase or a part of a fast movement to be slower, he can and would mark *un poco meno* or simply *meno mosso*—"a little less" or "less motion."

In the same way we can analyze other character indications, looking first for the original meaning of the word and then adapting it to the phrase in question. *Largamente* is another indication that can lead to false conclusions. It is very easy to play four or eight sixteenth notes "large, broad" in a relatively moving piece, let us say in an *Allegretto,* without altering the basic tempo. In the same way the intentions of other character indications (e.g., *con sentimento, slentando, morendo, smorzando*) can be implemented without changing the tempo.

One indication that seems to have been adopted and used erroneously by all composers is *Largo. Largo* means "large, broad," not "slow," but it is universally recognized as the slowest tempo, slower than *Lento* or *Adagio.* Even on the metronome it is given as the slowest tempo indication. Why this is so, nobody knows, but we have to accept that meaning. Several other Italian tempo markings have been misunderstood, and have acquired meanings that are similar, but slightly different, from their original sense.

Mainly for this reason, I think, and not because of strong nationalistic feelings, many composers began to mark their pieces in their own languages—Schumann and Hindemith in German, Ravel and Debussy in French. They also felt that the Italian words often have different meanings for different people. When Debussy writes *Assez vif et bien rhythmé,* in place of *Assai vivace, ben ritmico,* he knows it will be understood exactly, even by a child. Also, in his lifetime, French was more universally spoken in Europe than was Italian.

This short essay does not pretend to be a scientific study of all the character markings. Its goal is to call attention to the need to be more careful and exact in interpreting the indications in a musical composition. I have been aware, again and again over the years, that many musicians do not know the meanings of the tempo indications in the pieces they perform. The markings between the lines and between the notes are almost as important as the notes themselves. How can we interpret and reproduce a musical composition if we start out with false, or at least inaccurate, knowledge about the markings? We must not be too lazy or too proud to look up the exact meaning of a word in the dictionary, for our interpretations will be much better musically if we always read the composer's instructions carefully and translate them accurately.

Albert Lazan

A Few Moments of Beauty

Indiana University has a diverse string faculty: soloists, chamber music players, pedagogues, former concertmasters. In some cases their areas overlap, and all to the good. Our overall purpose is the same. Each of us pursues that elusive Greek, Orpheus. Happily, each in his own way.

Confine four of us in one room to discuss a piece of music, and chances are there will be a variety of concepts. We may differ on phrasing, fingerings, dynamics, tempi—no matter. Multiple ideas expose the inquiring student to a wider range, present him with choices. One hopes he will be forming his own opinion for the ultimate goal, a few moments of beauty.

Of course, without good technical application, there can be no beauty, no matter how admirable the musical intent. One needs to know how to move fluently, be it tennis or fiddling. Thus, when a student progresses to the point where he can turn a meaningful, imaginative phrase, my day is made.

How does a teacher go about having a student produce moments of beauty?

There is no one method or approach. Each student is different, physically and mentally, and it is up to the teacher to evaluate capabilities and to work accordingly. I have no magic pills, no pat innovations. To my way of thinking, nothing can take the place of talent, constructive daily practice, and "big" ears.

Awareness of intonation through intervals, chords, and keys must start with the first breath of the very first tone. The listening process never ceases, ears strung up like antennae and dictating to the brain each finger placement. A student will know that from B to C is a half-step. But how close? It will differ with the size of each finger. Only the ear is guide. Only the ear can measure and correct and demand clean pitch as well as a quality of sound.

Entering my studio for the first time, a student is subject to a "physical." As he plays for me, I probe, checking hand positions, finger action, bow strokes, string-crossings, shifting, vibrato. At the end of the session, I tell him, "My job as a teacher is to make my points clear. If there is something you fail to understand, say so, and I'll keep on lighting candles. But once you understand the problem and its remedy, it becomes your business to solve it. Fair enough?

"That means developing good practicing habits, which I cannot overstress, and which we shall be talking about frequently. In most cases you will be seeing me once a week; therefore you must teach yourself the other six days. Waiting for me to correct something that could have been done on your own is being lazy and wastes time. When a passage doesn't go, don't squander time in useless repetition. Pause for analysis. Revert to fundamentals. Practicing with thought and correct muscular conditions will result in improvement.

"Something else. Don't spend time on what you can already do. Concentrate on the troublesome places. At the end of the day, after the spadework, play through your assignments as a whole, noting what has stuck and what still comes unglued, and relegate the rough sections for additional work the next day.

"We deal," I inform the student, "with two elements: muscular control and musical perception. For the moment, I'd like to speak a little more about the physical.

"Like an athlete, an instrumentalist needs his daily dozen: scales, arpeggios, double-stops, and, very important, trill studies. Without doubt, trills are vital in developing good independent finger action. I think it unforgivable for a player to pass off a vibrato shake for a legitimate finger trill.

"Over the years, I have compiled a series of short exercises and excerpts, shifting, bowings, finger-extensions, all geared to the various problems that may come up. These are added to the daily dozen and played in different keys and rhythms, *and by rote*. With no printed page to get in the way, you can concentrate on your bow and left hand.

"Etudes and caprices are an integral part of the violin literature, and we shall be doing a variety. Most of them are attractive and beneficial, each with a special aim. Let me caution you again that dwelling too long on a single deficiency can become tiresome and dull the mind. Space your practicing, five minutes on a run in thirds, six minutes on a scratchy spiccato, and so on, returning to your problem during the course of the day with a fresher mind.

"I am not obsessed with calisthenics. I believe in doing only what is necessary to train your muscles. Unless there is a massive problem, I like to progress as soon as possible to the music itself, working on several contrasting pieces at a time. Diversified repertoire is refreshing and challenging, with each sonata, concerto, partita presenting its own style and difficulty. Thus, in blending musical thought and the correct use of muscles, you will be putting together factors that make for performance."

When the student leaves, I weigh his pluses and minuses. I ask myself, how will I open doors, expose him to song, show him the unlimited possibilities of musical expression? I must convey to him that notes in themselves are dormant ciphers on paper, each waiting to be roused, re-created, not by a robot who fires off a round of arpeggios, but by a thinking, flesh-and-blood player. Our medium is unique—a vibrating world of organized sound that includes shading, texture, pulsation; evokes nobility; projects a mood, a picture; embodies the full range of human emotions.

Untutored talent is an uncut gem that needs shaping and polishing. Emotions have to be re-defined. Beethoven is not Tchaikovsky, and that slide will never do. Sometimes an unruly temperament gets in the way. But when it works and the light catches, how rewarding!

A young violinist came to me for lessons. He was a meticulous player, well schooled, coordinated. He possessed a good ear. Unfortunately, he was inhibited. His expressive range was 2 on the Richter scale. His vibrato was without intensity, his phrasing without direction. One note was monotonously like the next. Technically, he needed to work on his bow arm, to use the stick more generously, to vary its speed, to improve his martelé. All of this, I prided myself, could be done. The big job was to bring him out. Somewhere must lurk a spark.

One day I called him on a particular phrase. Where was the music

going? What did it mean in terms of heartbeats? Style? Nuance? And
the section that followed? Why was he skimming across the strings
when it plainly called for a crescendo?

Later I listened to the Bach D minor Gigue. Did he think it was a
dirge? Where was the movement, the gaiety? I illustrated what I
meant. It was his turn to listen. Then I asked him to imitate. Because
he had an ear, his attempt was promising. "Go home and think about
it," I said. "Come back with some of your own lilt. I want people
dancing to that Gigue." There was a glimmer in his eye. It seemed
that I had finally gotten to him, made an impression, and I felt
encouraged.

The next lesson was a musical disaster. He was back to
neutral—and bloodless. It was disheartening. I began again. "For
heaven's sake, Mac, where's the verve, the pulse, the spirit? Get
that bow in the string and draw. Move it. Do something with it.
Don't simply stand there and noodle."

I could detect a resentment, even a small anger rising in him. Was
he losing his complacency? Was this progress at last? I was ruffling
him. Maybe that was exactly what he needed. "You have potential,"
I said more softly. "Here and there something nice peeps out. I want
more conviction, more vigor, more involvement. Exert yourself!
Project! If I didn't think you were capable, I wouldn't waste another
word."

I spent months cajoling, pleading, stirring him up, demanding that
he play in phrases, emphasizing the notes he thought the composer
intended to be emphasized. It was so obviously written in the music.
I made weekly tapes of his progress. For the first time he began
listening to himself objectively. The music, he now realized, had
been mainly in his belly. He would have to present it, deliver it on a
platter. It was a totally new concept for him. He realized that there
was nothing personal in my criticism, and if sometimes my words
were caustic, my only desire was for meaningful music. At his
Senior Recital I had my reward. His playing had fine moments, even
some beauty. In the Chausson *Poème,* a touch of artistry.

I tell my students that every worthy musician tries to find the
composer's intent. That intent may be interpreted in many ways. No
two individuals see, hear, feel exactly alike. The same piece played

by Heifetz and Kreisler may be as dissimilar as the men themselves. Like it or not, musical performance ends up being personal. Dynamics become personal. So can tempi. Yehudi Menuhin once said, "The whole beauty of the violin is you make your sound in your own image—your strengths, weaknesses, flexibilities, the way your blood flows, your temperament—that is you. I always wanted music to speak. I wanted the listener to say, 'Ah, yes, that is true.' I didn't just want to play the violin. I wanted to say something."

In speaking of intent, I like to single out Beethoven's String Quartet Op. 95. The first movement is marked *Allegro con brio*. How lively? How *brio*? Beethoven hands us a metronome marking, but the drama is left to the players. What do the initial eleven notes mean in terms of human expression? Can a two-measure statement result in clenched fists, a universal outcry of defiance?

I am asked, "How far up the creative ladder is the performing musician? Hasn't it all been indicated by the composer?"

"Like a map," I concur. "A composer notates a musical journey. A player studies it. Depending on his insight, he imbues the score with some of his own salt and pepper. The more profound his insight, the greater the artist."

Shoptalk with a group of students: "A beautiful vibrato," I quote Albert Spalding, "is one that sounds the note and lowers it rhythmically and quickly." Except for reasons of color or emphasis, the oscillation should not be of the stop-and-go variety, "purling" one note and dropping the other, but a rhythmic, continuous pulsation so that the tone is even. Also, it must be quick enough so that the ear will not detect the altered pitch.

Either a wrist or an arm vibrato or a combination of both can produce engaging results if the first joint of each finger remains flexible. If that joint is locked, prohibiting a rocking motion, the vibrato will sound tight and brittle. Warning: avoid using solely a finger vibrato; it can promise only a bleak future.

I firmly believe that a captivating vibrato is part of one's talent. The natural player gives it innate sheen and luster, varies its speed, sprinkles and stirs and whips up the right consistency to enhance the musical demands. Such a vibrato cannot be acquired any more than talent can be learned. I like to think of vibrato as musical seasoning, lifting and bringing out the full flavor of a phrase. The bow shades; the vibrato adds bouquet.

We finger for color and clarity, and in rapid passages to have the hand cover as many notes as possible without shifting. Our fingers are not webbed feet, and that brings up extensions. About 1751, Francesco Geminiani wrote a treatise on violin playing, the source of modern-day extensions. The ability to stretch left-hand fingers in either direction is a real advantage in negotiating awkward passages. Flexibility between fingers can eliminate unnecessary shifting, and make for smoother playing. "Let your fingers do the walking."

William Primrose once made a fascinating remark: "Think of the fingerboard as one area, one position."

In the early seventeenth century, the perfection of the violin played no small part in the unprecedented development of purely instrumental music, particularly the Italian solo violin sonata. When great luthiers placed superb instruments in the hands of talented composer-violinists, the Baroque period, Italian style, became one of the most fruitful and inventive in musical history. Men like Vivaldi, Veracini, Locatelli, Tartini, to name but a few, began presenting obstacle courses, raising the level of violin playing to a degree previously unknown. Modern-day violinists are still meeting their challenges, especially when it comes to the unaccompanied works of a German colleague and finger-twister, J.S. Bach.

Twentieth-century artist-teachers have updated the sound principles of the past with excellent results. Witness some of their well-taught students. I believe that there is more erudite teaching and guidance now than ever before. State universities have to a large extent become the modern temples where many top musicians gather. In some ways, American institutions have made this a golden age of music.

We are also in the space age, and velocity has become the order of the day. I remember when high speed was ten miles an hour in Mama's electric car—and the same concerto was programmed year after year. Now we do five of them in a season, and if an Allegro movement has a metronome mark of 100 to the quarter note, we double it! Happily, not all of it is sensation. The musical level of our recitals is high and sophisticated. "Poster" music has become an endangered species. Through recordings, tapes, and television we have been exposed to the finest in music. Imagine "standing room only" for an all-Beethoven program!

I have a pet gripe, public school music. In many cases, it hasn't kept pace with the times. The essentials of technique should be achieved in the grade and high schools, during the formative years when muscles are pliable. It is here that our fine instrumentalists and teachers should be. Often we have a jack-of-all-trades teaching all the strings. One word will cover this deplorable situation. Malpractice!

I find it criminal to see talented students entering college with impaired bow arms, faulty left-hand positions, rigid thumbs and wrists. Our studios must not turn into first-aid stations. Instead of handling emergency cases, we teachers should be administering Beethoven, Bartók, and Mozart.

The educational system needs airing. We need airing. A start has been made. Degrees must be geared to meet the situation. The Master of Strings, which trains the student properly on all stringed instruments, looks promising. Concerning our part in the venture, the better we prepare a B.M.E. student as a player, musician, and future teacher, the better staffed our public schools will be.

"Must it be? It must be!"

Having been a member of a professional string quartet for nearly two decades, I would be remiss were I to omit some discussion of chamber music. No serious student dare do without it. It opens eyes, ear, mind. It develops the listening process, instrumental control, and musicianship more than any experience I know. It also happens to comprise some of the most rewarding literature in the world. What a unique blend of musical thought and expression! It's no accident that Beethoven created seventeen masterpieces for the string quartet.

I am invariably asked about the role of the second violinist. Add the viola and make it "the inner voices." They're the manipulators. They roll out the carpet for the main voice, become the accompanying playmates, the vibrato matchers, the intonation adjusters. After noodling for half a page, the spotlight suddenly falls on one of them to produce the great sum of one solo phrase. Then, presto, back to the blender.

I can now report that the day of the inner voices has dawned. Beethoven began feeding them some fine morsels in his quartets. Brahms gave the viola a lush piece of fruit in his B-flat opus. Prokofiev presented the second violinist with a bonanza in his Second Quartet. With contemporary composers on the scene, the inner voices are at last emancipated.

"But," one may ask, "what of the um-pahs? Someone has to play them." True, but the era of the old-world court is over. Today, professional string players are better equipped, more knowledgeable. In most cases, the two violinists in a quartet are equally skilled. Even distribution among the instruments is here.

Looking back, I smile. There are a few nagging thoughts. Can four diverse players make love at the same time to the same mistress, music? From a personal angle, just how realistic is the quartet medium? Can four musicians with dissimilar styles, techniques, temperaments, and philosophies achieve true unity? Symphonic players are whipped into line by the conductor. Members of a string quartet are in a way free souls, each with his own bias and the option to state it. I think of a quartet not as a choir of angels but merely as four humans held together by the greatness of the music.

In summing up, let me say that I strive for a relationship between a student and myself in which we learn from each other; in which we build regard and mutual respect, no matter what our shortcomings. It is always a joy for me to cultivate a student's love for music, and for him to understand in depth the meaning of music through the ages. And when he graduates, he may leave, I hope, with an inquiring mind, always seeking a few moments of beauty.

Fritz Magg

Cello Sounds of Today

The cello has existed in its present size and shape for almost three hundred years. Modern concave bows have been in use for about two centuries. The transition from the viola da gamba to the cello as a solo stringed instrument, encompassing a range from the bass to the soprano register, was virtually completed by the middle of the eighteenth century. What, then, can be said that is peculiar to the 1970s about the sound to be coaxed from a musical instrument so long in use, so thoroughly explored and exposed?

I do not intend in this essay to attempt a compilation or to suggest the best cellistic realization of the numerous new sound effects with which contemporary composers try to enrich their color schemes. The devices are many, some representing only modifications and some real innovations, some being mere gimmicks and some essential to a new musical language. It seems to me to be premature to classify them according to the prospects of their being of lasting value. I have not encountered any effects so radically new in technique as to require prolonged separate study. Their difficulties concern for the most part the player's ability to decipher the sometimes quite complex tables of instructions on unconventional ways of plucking and bowing the string or redefining portamento, vibrato, and fractional pitches or asking for percussive sounds on and off the fingerboard. Most of this can be learned quite readily, and the composer's indications can be carried out faithfully in letter and in spirit as long as the resulting wear and tear on bow hair and strings does not force the player into bankruptcy, and a beautiful cello's varnish, which may have lasted in all its original glory for centuries, is not damaged in the process. In any event, it is not the tricks that will be important ultimately but the spirit that they are supposed to clarify or enhance. And it is this *Zeitgeist,* the spiritual meaning of our time, that so far has occurred in too many styles and with too much inconsistency in notation to allow us to arrive at anything but a personal value judgment of what will survive and what will fall by the wayside. One does not view a storm most objectively from its vortex.

What I consider more useful here is an assessment of the mechanics and esthetics of cello sounds as they are, or might be, heard in our day and age relative to that large body of music written between 1750 and 1950, which makes up the bulk of the current concert repertoire. In addition to those two centuries, I shall discuss Bach in some detail; the style of his works demands its own technical solutions. At the other end, the string music of the last 25 years, as noted above, is still following too many unpredictable paths to be included here. But from Haydn to Bartók, cello playing has developed quite organically. Numerous and momentous changes in musical esthetics have called for new instrumental attitudes, virtuosity, timbres, and accents, but cello technique was already established to a great extent when radical musical changes took place. Being able to play Beethoven's Great Fugue well is instrumentally surprisingly relevant to a successful performance of Schoenberg's Fourth String Quartet. If you can master Schubert's "Arpeggione" Sonata, a Milhaud concerto ought not faze you. Where, on the other hand, the cellistic problems are rather special, as in Kodály's solo sonata, nothing but a specific analysis will do. Observations of a general applicability would seem more appropriate in this essay, which does not purport to deal with the question "How do today's cello compositions sound?" but with "What sounds may one expect from today's cellists?" There are at least three basic reasons why such an assessment from the vantage point of the 1970s would differ significantly from one made prior to the rather sharp dividing line of World War II.

To begin with, factionalism according to nationalities and separate schools of cello doctrine is rapidly diminishing. Just as the astronauts were able to view the Earth a few years ago for the first time as an unbroken entity, so the conquest of space through radio, television, worldwide availability of the same records, and the easing of

traveling conditions have created a unified stage on which the leading artists are on constant display everywhere. Likewise, many students, aided by various grants, have ceased to regard distance as a
hindrance in seeking out their favorite places of study. A school like
ours at Indiana University is filled with young people from all continents. The proverbial melting pot of New York City is now found
operating happily not only here in Bloomington but in any place
where artist–teachers are able to nourish the imagination of students
who had heard them perform in person or on records or had met
them in master classes around the globe. Furthermore, a significant
redistribution of artistic talent has accompanied the mass migrations
taking place around the time of World War II. And new focal points
of cultural activity have attained global importance in places like
Israel and Japan, which not only have contributed to the pedagogic
knowledge of the musical world at large but also continue to send a
stream of enormously gifted students to the centers of musical
studies.

Small wonder, then, that a constantly expanding process of inter-
nationalization is taking place among artists and students
everywhere. Whereas up to the 1940s some artists could be labeled
quite readily on the basis of national idiosyncrasies, today the differences are more and more the result of individual temperaments
rather than the product of climate and schooling. Some ensembles,
especially orchestras with long, distinguished traditions, still retain
these vanishing regional characteristics collectively, although one
finds even in them considerably more heterogeneous elements than
heretofore. But what of the old clichés associating American music
making with fast and glossy, French with elegant and glib, German
with ponderous, Italian with cantilena-obsessed, etc.? Often enough
they had no validity, anyway, when they concerned some of the
great creative musicians—how glib is Berlioz, how ponderous
Mozart? Now such associations are becoming ever more obsolete
with regard to performers, too, and will be completely meaningless
when the artists straddling the mid-century have disappeared. As a
result, the successful cellist of today may well continue to display a
special stylistic affinity to certain types of compositions. But in
terms of what constitutes good cello playing, he will have to be able
to travel on an internationally valid artistic passport.

Secondly, there are the acoustical problems of today's performances to be considered. I imagine that at the beginning of the cello's soloistic existence, Boccherini played in about the same light way at his public concerts as in the environment of the salon. His manner of holding the bow, as depicted in his portraits, seems to preclude any weightiness in his style of playing. Even as concert halls grew larger, a single manner of projection for all locations, at least in solo recitals, may have held true well into the beginning of the twentieth century, when the world's most renowned string players still played for audiences of only a few hundred people in such illustrious places as Vienna's Boesendorfersaal and London's Wigmore Hall. But today's performers have to be ready routinely for the differences in sound production demanded by the extremes of hypersensitive modern microphones, on the one hand, and cavernous halls, seating several thousand people, on the other. (I am not thinking here of London's Albert Hall and New York City's Madison Square Garden, which occasionally house a misplaced string soloist, but of what has become the average main auditorium in one of the new art centers.) Many great string players have commented on the dualism of performance this necessitates: giving the requisite amplitude of volume and phrasing to their playing in large halls, while avoiding excesses of any kind before the microphone. The first obviously invites looking for a forcefulness inimical to the stringed instrument's limited capacity for loudness, "forceful" turning into "forced" and strident, and the scientifically unsound effort becoming counterproductive. The fear of not being heard involves, moreover, the great danger of monotony: unrelieved loud playing, with the same gorgeous vibrato, the same heavy bow pressure, and the same emoting pretty soon amount to the same dullness. Monotony also lurks at the other end: the taboos before the microphone all too easily shift the emphasis from achievement to avoidance and result in overly careful, sometimes technically unobjectionable but expressively bland performances, which crop up on recordings in all musical media. Perhaps there is less cause for worry on this score today than in the cool 1950s. The ever-changing winds of musical taste currently seem to be veering from the Apollonian toward the Dionysian.

Although these problems of sound production have been

especially aggravating for cellists, who have an inherent difficulty in projecting low-pitched passages with clarity and power, they seem to have turned out to be a blessing in disguise. Imaginative cellists have known for a long time that it is just as shortsighted not to develop the maximal tonal capacity of their instruments as to use it all the time. But the contradictory demands of very large halls and of electronic sensitivity have forced them into ever more critical listening and the discovery that optimum sound benefits little from scraping and crunching; that it is rather the unconditionally focused, freely vibrating sound that helps their playing to be potent. Today's audiences will no longer let flimsy or scratchy sounds go unchallenged just because they are, as a rule, to be expected from a cello. It has, therefore, become the unavoidable concern of every professional cellist to divest himself of old cellistic habits of sliding around on the fingerboard and using unsupported, stifling bow strokes. He must learn to produce notes that immediately establish with fullness and clarity their dead center, whether it be with a viola da gamba's lightness in mind or with the sonorities appropriate to Prokofiev's *Sinfonia Concertante*. Failure to achieve this will make a cellist appear anachronistically clumsy before the microphone and unintelligible in the concert hall.

This challenge and the very happy way in which it is being met nowadays lead me to point number three in the appraisal of current cello playing: the undeniable fact that many more cellists play the cello superbly than ever before. It goes without saying that there must have been at all times a few outstanding cellists who performed at the highest level conceivable at their time. Their extraordinary talent simply enabled them to play much better than most of their fellow cellists. Such a feat does not seem to suffice today. The broad base of cello playing is so very high that it is no longer a question of excelling by being outstanding just by cellistic standards; today the cellist must be able to match the accuracy and fluency of a top-level violinist note for note. The previously mentioned factor of focusing the sound plays a great role. A well-focused sound has presence, body, and carrying power and also offers the best opportunity for discerning whether the demands of good timing and pitch have been met. And here is where the crux of the improvement lies: cellists today produce not only cleaner bow strokes but also a much higher percentage of the right pitches at the right time.

The ability to define the correct pitch, instantly, frees the playing finger from heaviness during the remainder of the note and right away offers three great benefits that extend far beyond the satisfaction of smoothly working mechanics to the realm of Art itself: first, the intrinsic beauty of finely honed pitch; second, the possibility of individualized articulation in the left hand by means of a constantly shifting weight, from the daring firmness of initiating a pitch to the utmost lightness in moving away from it, a differentiation indispensable for the clear enunciation of every note and for a vibrato adaptable in width and speed; and, finally, the restriction of the portamento to being an expressive device instead of a cumbersome means of transportation.

Good pitch depends on many factors: obviously, on familiarity with the map of the fingerboard; also on an aptly placed, compact left hand; on the supple use of the left arm in carrying the hand to the right places without tension; on the aforementioned individualization of finger weight; when shifts coincide with bow changes, on good coordination between the two arms; on constant readiness to correct a faulty finger placement so quickly that the change is not perceived as a separate action. But even when all these conditions are fulfilled reasonably well, the most important factor, it seems to me, is the acute *expectation* of the coming note. This means a sensation encompassing a keen anticipation of its pitch, of its placement within an independently known hand position, and of the timing and nature of whatever arm movement is necessary to reach or shift toward it. I cannot readily believe that more cellists play in tune now because of better ears or fingers in our time. It must be a little like the breakthrough in the four-minute mile. Once Mr. Bannister had conquered not only the stopwatch but also the psychological barrier, in a rather short time several others achieved the previously impossible. Perhaps it was Casals who demonstrated that, with extraordinary talent and diligence, consistently good pitch on the cello was possible if one expected it and fought for it. So the dream of playing in tune was raised from wishful thinking to the reality of a goal already reached by another. And now the achievement is just as difficult as ever but not as rare, and the unwary public is callous enough to demand not only clean bow sounds but good intonation as a commonplace.

Here we are, then, with better-functioning cellists in great numbers. In string quartets they are able to make even their C-strings respond in time to match the attacks of the higher instruments. They can produce basses that are reliable foundations for chordal tuning and passages in high registers that do not sound awkward next to those of their colleagues. In the orchestra they can give a fiery conductor all the warmth of expression he asks for and produce the lean articulation demanded by a precisionist. Young players are hardly fazed by rapidly changing time signatures, skip nimbly through the erstwhile feared *Rite of Spring,* and are remarkably secure in the much greater complexities that confront them in contemporary works. Of course, there seems to be no end in sight for how much more razor-sharp their rhythms will have to become. Much of the very essence of "Third Stream" music, for example, would be lost without the most meticulous timing. But sometimes I ask, *Quo vadis, compositore?* I know that some of Brahms's syncopations used to be difficult, and then came the rhythmic intricacies of Ravel and Stravinsky and Schoenberg and Carter, and they were all mastered in due time. But if a really precise performance of 13 against 22 is wanted, why not give it to a computer? *It* won't have any trouble.

I am considerably less charmed by the lack of rhythmic discipline displayed by some young cellists in older soloistic compositions. A lack of stylistic awareness may account for a performance of a Haydn concerto that has neither a basic tempo nor exact rhythms. But with all of our vaunted technique, is it not more likely to be mental inertia than muscular awkwardness that prevents a cellist from playing dotted rhythms correctly, particularly those within a triple meter, like ♩♩♩ ? Failure to synchronize a passage like Ex. 1, at the beginning of the Dvořák Concerto, with the orchestral passage in Ex. 2 seems as sloppy to me as scratching or playing out of tune.

Ex. 1

Ex. 2

After finding so much to praise, I see that I am drifting from discussing the cello sounds as they *are* heard in our day to the ones that *might* be heard. Having gone so far in developing the potential of cello technique, for what further purpose should we now use our achievements? At a time when life is so free of conventions and regulations, what fascination can the discipline of our art hold? Where instant gratification is the watchword of the day, what beacon may be lighted by infinite patience on the way toward a cherished goal?

The answer for me is the same as the one which made me choose my profession in the first place, which has made me enjoy it year in and year out, which has kept me laboring at better understanding and improved skills in spite of the never-ending search, the professional frustrations, and the utter lack of assurance of ever having mastered the definitive. It is simply this: the reward has justified the effort. It started with a hope and grew into the conviction that what I am doing is time well spent, the prize worth waiting and fighting for. It is the intoxicating love that I have for a piece like Beethoven's Op. 131 that makes boundless patience a joy, the fascination with its workmanship that precludes disenchantment, the reverence for its creator's lofty status that mandates the utmost discipline and perseverance in its service.

Not many compositions have the worth of Op. 131, to be sure, but there are hundreds of others that are similarly capable of recharging the vitality of the cellist at every turn, keeping him loving and fascinated. It may mean participation in a glorious piece of chamber music here, in a resplendent symphony there, shining as a soloist or being an indispensable contributor in an operatic production. If the player will just give himself up to the excitement of a piece in all its aspects, its beauty will not pall and the ugly specter of routine will not kill his joy.

Reverence for the composer's wishes is another matter. In the orchestra, the cellist is subject to the discipline of a section under the watchful eye of the conductor. In small ensembles, the alert ears of one's colleagues will keep one honest. Later I would like to discuss a few instances, however, in which the cellist performs under conditions of maximal initiative and responsibility, and state concretely what I mean by faithfulness to the composer and how the cello might sound if the attitude of goodwill toward the composition were always the fountainhead of one's labors.

But first a few general observations are in order for the benefit of those rugged individualists who feel that their artistry is not sufficiently challenged by having to make myriad decisions on tempi and their fluctuations, on balancing sonorities, on emphases and nuances, which even carefully marked scores leave unspecified. They are always clamoring naively for the freedom to express *themselves* before they have absorbed a composer's ideas and can act, freely and cocreatively, as a catalyst of his music.

Goodwill toward the composition—the German composer Hans Pfitzner thought this subject of sufficient importance to make that selfsame phrase ("Der Wille zum Werk") the focal point of his book *Werk und Wiedergabe*. But how relevant is it in our time? I have met all sorts of composers, from the liberal ones ("Anything you wish to do is all right with me") to the stern ones ("I wrote down what I wanted and don't need to have anyone's personal viewpoint added"). Between these extremes I would hope for an interpreter with the basic willingness to function on a plane congenial with the composer's grand design and, insofar as that is possible and essential, to obey detailed instructions as well. But suppose he is unwilling to undertake this basic commitment. Suppose that not only musicians declared their artistic independence but editors rewrote old books, poems, plays; suppose every work of art were in the public domain to be altered at will. This is what might happen:

A museum decides to commission an illustrious painter to produce a replica of one of the world's most famous frescoes, *The Last Supper* by Leonardo da Vinci, because not everyone can travel to Milan to see the original. The artist, justifiably proud of his craftsmanship and his powers of imagination, has no intention of delivering a photographic copy. He finds Leonardo's formal design somewhat old-fashioned and decides to move the figure of Christ from dead center to the side, placing the characteristic figure of St.

Peter more toward the middle. This necessitates cutting off one apostle at the end, a minor matter considering the advantage that the all too obvious halo effect of Christ's head against the bright window in the background has now been removed. After all, nobody uses a dove in the last scene of *Parsifal* anymore, nor would anyone be so amateurishly literal as to put a lilac bush on the stage when Hans Sachs sings his heart out about its sweet fragrance.

Some members of the board of directors of the museum are disturbed by the willfulness of the painter, but his draftsmanship is immaculate and his colors are so much more brilliant than the fading ones on the refectory wall of Santa Maria delle Grazie. So they give in.

Time magazine devotes a lengthy article to "The Case of the Missing Apostle." It points out that historically there were twelve, not eleven, disciples; that Leonardo based his whole design on creating four groups of three apostles each, with the resigned figure of the lonely Christ in the middle. Nobody mentions that after five hundred years Leonardo may still have a copyright on his work.

But a painting is, of course, so much more definitive than a score can ever be. When it is finished it is there for all time in only one form, and only a vandal would tamper with it. Music, however, is forever flexible. Beethoven probably presented his pieces differently every time he re-created them. So do every mature musician's performances vary, dictated by a different pulse, an altered environment, the desire for a new emphasis. But how far may these deviations go? When does a legitimate new perspective turn into a silly ego trip?

We are in a class on symphonic literature. The professor is lecturing on the "Eroica" with eloquence and wit and an endless stream of "don't you see?" Not since "The Emperor's New Clothes" has anyone been able to make so much visible that was not there. He expostulates on the two opening chords: "These two loud crashes of sound, don't you see, are quite out of harmony with the sinuous character of the melody starting in the third measure. But you must understand that it was necessary for Beethoven, in front of a gathering of aristocratic amateurs, to halt their disrespectful chatter with an attention-commanding gesture. Having shocked them into silence, he could proceed with gentler sounds. Today we have much better-behaved audiences. The two introductory chords, if they are needed at all, should be brought into line with what follows, don't you see? Two arpeggiated string chords with perhaps a touch of sustained high woodwinds would be so much more musical. You could not do this in Boston's Symphony Hall, of course; Beacon Hill audiences are so conservative. But it has been tried with great success by the Attaboya Philharmonic. The music critic there raved about never having felt closer to the true spirit of Beethoven.''

Absurd. Utterly absurd, figments of some wild imagination, the missing apostle and the civilized "Eroica." Everybody knows these masterworks and no one could get away with these "improvements." But how much more absurd than, in a lesser-known composition, Schumann's Cello Concerto, turning the transition from the second to the last movement, which is logically marked "faster and faster," into a majestic ritardando? Where was the outcry by the music critics when one of our most beloved artists committed what could not be called anything but a mortal sin? Didn't they care about anything but sweet fluency? Didn't they know the difference? Because it is here that the answer to respect for the creative mind lies: to know what is written; even, one hopes, to understand why it was written that way; and to care enough to ask oneself humbly every time one contemplates a change whether one really knows better.

Obviously, an attempt at textual fidelity does not guarantee an eloquent performance any more than any other form of accuracy does. But it is often an indispensable prerequisite to ultimate success and always an initial moral obligation.

Now to some concrete examples from the core of the cellist's repertoire by the three Bs.

Let us start with Bach. I have heard some cellists talk in a derogatory way about Haydn quartets or Beethoven sonatas or Schumann or Brahms, tearing down in turn just about all the gods that one would think unassailable. But every cellist, without exception, loves the Bach suites, *must* play them, and is profoundly convinced that no other cellist has fathomed their essence. How is it to be found?

Many good and wise people have written thousands of words about what is in good or bad taste in the interpretation of Bach, which of his pieces are freely rhapsodic or strict in rhythm, which are to be viewed as holy altarpieces or as products of his lively humanity. It is easy enough to agree on certain traits of Bach, such as his ever-present awareness of the Deity and the orderliness in his music that this implies. But when one wishes to define his style, it becomes apparent again and again that this most readily dissected genius is the most difficult one to pin down. With Bach, as with every composer, one must come to grips with a basic definition of what befits his style and what must be excluded. With some composers we feel quite at ease in assembling such a list of characteristics. A recent record jacket quotes Mr. Rostropovich as having expressed his deepest feeling of identification with the music of Tchaikovsky. I might say a similar thing about myself with regard to Schubert. Another person may profess a special affinity to Stravinsky. But Bach is so remote in time and the magnitude of his works so extraordinary that no one may claim him as his own. As I think of the disagreement that even the utterances of such luminaries of yesteryear as Landowska and Casals evoke nowadays, I just wish to thank those two giants devoutly for the tremendous involvement and skill with which they have contributed to our knowledge and appreciation of Bach; but then I must keep on searching for "The Truth" according to my own lights.

To understand the *structure* of Bach's cello suites, one need but turn to the painstaking analysis by Diran Alexanian. A little later I shall discuss their *language* and how this language might live in our day. But as to the *esthetic* of the suites, the history of Bach interpretation seems to mandate that every faction be permitted to produce its own share of scholars and visionaries. If this results, as it always has, in performances of the cello suites so radically at variance that they can barely be recognized as the same pieces, this might turn out to be quite harmless: we would have five hundred different versions of the suites but since they are masterpieces of a unique kind, the cat would probably always land on its feet, no matter from what height it was dropped. Except there is, alas, this drawback: it is sad but true that the uninitiated general public all too often views the appearance of the cello suites on recital programs with marked suspicion. How can something so widely revered evoke so little love? How can the term *uninitiated* include in this case a super-musician like Toscanini, who asked Piatigorsky in all earnestness why he was programming such awful music? My theories on this run along these lines: just as the aforementioned Haydn concerto will not succeed when one takes it out of its style, so this mass of black notes, which make up the Bachian dance movements, will not speak to naive audiences when not rendered in their original language. Hamlet in Edwardian clothes, Romeo addressing Juliet as "you" are of interest only to those theatergoers whose surfeit of standard Shakespeare makes them crave new sensations at all costs. For a naiver audience, the original is more poetic and therefore more appealing.

In the case of Bach's cello suites, a departure from the Baroque language of alternating détaché strokes with brief legatos toward an indiscriminate slurring means, in my opinion, such a loss of rhythmic vitality that the tepid waves of unrelieved or arbitrarily interrupted legato should by rights put everyone to sleep; only the solemn and unquestioning awe with which the suites are regarded by the connoisseurs can act as a preventive. In those smoothened renditions the love for the composer is certainly fervid and the fascination with his mastery intense; but the reverence for his markings is minimal. Some reasons for such a lack of faithfulness are quite obvious: First, there is no original manuscript by Bach extant, in contrast to the violin sonatas and partitas, for which Bach's calligraphically immaculate manuscripts present a compelling point of departure for all "interpretations." (Incidentally, I would like to suggest to those people who maintain that the manuscript usually attributed to his second wife, Anna Magdalena, was in fact written by Bach himself, that no composer would make the kind of mistakes—so many obviously wrong notes, parts of phrases omitted altogether, the word "Courante" written as the heading for an Allemande—to which a copyist is prone.) Second, the early copies of the cello suites differ in bowings and even in pitches. (Some, but not all that much. Only in the fugato section of the C minor Prelude do I find phrasings that seem so haphazard that I feel forced to adopt a logic borrowed from Bach's works with analogous structures. Where the copies do not enlighten us about every detail, the knowledge of Bach's bowing practice gained from the Brandenburg Concertos, orchestral suites, violin partitas and concertos, and cantatas ought to make a choice of stylistically acceptable solutions possible.) Third, and perhaps most important, it is difficult to make short détaché strokes in low registers speak freely on the cello and to combine them into unbroken phrases. All of these have contributed to an attitude of "anything goes."

If, by contrast, a hundred violinists were to perform the beginning of the Allemande in Bach's D minor Partita, there probably would not be a single one who would slur the six sixteenth notes from the e to the c sharp in the first measure of Ex. 3.

Ex. 3

Bach marked them detached and that is how they are played, distinct from the legato of the following groups of two and three notes. Immediately the grave spaciousness of the movement is documented, and the listener can say happily to himself: I can see what this music is all about. I am willing to bet that most cellists would slur these notes, presumably to help the smooth forward motion of the phrase, as they do in *their* D minor Allemande. Here all the manuscripts of Anna Magdalena Bach, Kellner, and Westphal show clearly a great many phrasings of two slurred sixteenths (♫) , which help to determine the mood of *this* Allemande equally convincingly and represent, incidentally, a bowing very common in Baroque and early classical music. But ever so many cellists choose to use an overall legato. It is easier. It has the negative virtue of avoiding potentially clumsy bow changes. But smoothness, so often desirable in a physical sense, can sometimes turn out to be a superficial and boring trait, in music as in people.

If a Toscanini was perhaps put off not only by a lack of rhythmic incisiveness but also by unappealing cello sounds, I can sympathize with his distaste: these suites have long suffered from floundering between the Scylla of swishy sounds and the Charybdis of scratchy ones. But if my optimism regarding present-day bow control is justified, that does not need to be the case anymore.

To begin with, it ought to be established—*before* one concerns oneself with the very controversial problem of stresses and groupings in Bach—that "a phrase is a phrase is a phrase," governed by immutable laws of harmonic progression and melodic structure, applicable to music of any time. If we cannot play phrases as cohesive entities we shall not make music. In terms of cello mechanics this means that for as long as the breath of the phrase lasts without interruption, the motion of the bow arm ought not be stopped. However many bow strokes a phrase may encompass, continuous motion and smoothly anticipated new bow angles and levels can give the illusion of an endless breath. If the demands of articulation and phrasing, on the other hand, ask for the separation of certain sounds within the phrase, we have to devise ways of achieving this, not by stopping the bow, except where an outright staccato effect is in order, but by diminuendos, to a zero pressure where necessary. One simply has to learn to keep the two functions of drawing and of pressing independent of each other. The beautifully defined gamba strokes, so characteristic of Baroque articulation, which move on the heavy beats from the tip on down and work with bow-speed accents rather than with pressure accents, have to be transformed into a mechanism suitable to the bigger sonorities required by larger halls. This is quite feasible by assigning to the bow a permanent function as an integral part of the bow arm, to be carried at will into contact and out of contact with the string. In this way one can use as much bow and stay on the string as long and as firmly as the situation demands without becoming "rosin-bound," like a fly on flypaper. Only in very rapid détaché strokes can the bow be led back and forth in close contact with the string without the risk of stickiness or a lack of definition.

Moreover, the liveliest left-hand articulation ought to be used in the performance of the suites. While this music offers the opportunity and, indeed, the necessity of practicing the most meticulous legato style in both arms—involuntary portato ought to be avoided like the plague!—I would suggest that the initial phase of left-hand practice consist of a totally individualized vibrato on every note, for the benefit of clarity, evenness, and intonation. Personally I would be just as happy never to hear any shifts in the fast movements of the suites. Anyone who thinks he *has* to use a slide should ask himself honestly not only how such a practice is regarded now but, especially in the case of a recording, how he is going to like it a few years hence.

The playing of double-stops and chords, the quality of which is of paramount importance in the rendition of Bach's works for solo violin, is much less prominent in the cello suites. They do seem to be problematic in the Sixth Suite, however, and earlier in such isolated movements as the first Gavotte of the Fifth Suite. Since their use increases in later compositions for solo cello, such as works by Reger, Hindemith, and Britten, and most recent cello literature is full of them, one might mention here that their appearance is often noticed with dismay in otherwise satisfactory performances. While I have suggested before that, with a very finely trained ear, the antici-pation of coming pitches can make the fingers sniff out the right places on the fingerboard like hunting dogs a scent (let anyone who believes he can always hit the right pitches without the help of the ear try recording himself with his ears plugged up), the possibility of minute adjustments is considerably curtailed in multiple stops. Cor-rections seem to be more difficult when two or more fingers are pressing down instead of only one.

Playing double-stops in tune requires a perfect visualization of a position plus the constant insistence on hearing the resultant pitches, called "Tartini's tones." But not only the pitch of double-stops is frequently inferior to that of single notes, but their vibrancy as well. How very rare is the cellist who can make them truly sing in the cadenza of Shostakovich's First Concerto! And rarer still, perhaps, is one whose double-stops enhance a musical line instead of interrupting it. In this department, cellists have a long way to go to catch up with the achievements of the best violinists, such as the thrilling glow of Fritz Kreisler's double-stops.

As to chords, on the other hand, the lower and more expansive sonorities ought to make life easier for the cellist than for the vio-linist, as long as he avoids clutching the bow too tightly, directs his energy at firmly stroking the string instead, and follows the curve of the bridge steadily. Particularly in Bach I dislike the sharp break from the bass to the top note of a chord. Emulating the roundness of an arpeggiated pizzicato chord and using a middle note as a connect-ing link between low and high can do much to increase the resonance and fluency of chord playing.

Empirically speaking, the fusion of sounds of the cello and the piano is not easy to achieve. The problem is not insoluble if the cello

sounds are clear and firm and the piano touch remains limpid. I do
not mean to suggest in the least that I favor flaccid piano playing in
partnership with a cello, but some concepts must remain exceed-
ingly flexible. It seems particularly necessary here to strive for the
most lucid presentation of the score, stripped of instrumental
fetishes, because amalgamation by the two instruments is much
more difficult to achieve, even by quite sensitive musicians, than by
an ensemble within the string family, where mutual reactions will be
more automatic. Here, as everywhere, the conquest of a composition ought to start with a definition of its character in one's mind,
from the whole on to the large sections and down to the details,
followed by an attempt to find the appropriate technical means of
carrying out these concepts. To bring them to life and to create a
harmonious whole of a cello and piano ensemble will involve a redefining not only of dynamics but of legato, staccato, accents, and
even tempo. Each player may feel he has hit upon the meaning
perfectly suited to his instrument, but now the two need to be ac-
commodated. Some samples from the sonata literature may help to
clarify this point more succinctly than would piano trios, quartets,
and quintets. In the latter the writing is predominantly antiphonal
between the piano and the strings, and the problems of meshing and
balancing all sounds are often much easier to solve.

Let us first consider the nature of cello–piano melody with an
example by Beethoven. The main theme of the first movement in his
Sonata in A major, Op. 69, can be very beautifully realized on the
piano through the bell-like quality of all the unhurried half, quarter,
and eighth notes (see Ex. 4).

Ex. 4

Even though the pianist cannot resort to some of the expressive devices available to the cellist, the effect can be very songful and touching. The cello, which precedes the piano with the same melody, ought to operate, it seems to me, in the same framework of expression. The piece is too young at this time to make a virtue of contrasting styles. The piano's instrumental realization ought to be anticipated in the cello's noble and clear tone production. Only a cellist interested exclusively in his own sensualism and unconcerned with the structure of the composition will claim the right to use fat slides and a luscious vibrato here and let the pianist fend for himself. In contrast, I would take the cue for the melody of the last movement's introductory Adagio, where the theme is introduced by the piano, from the cello's natural warmth.

Ex. 5

The inward expressiveness so typical of Beethoven can here unite the cantabile statements of both instruments in a beguiling linkup of sonorities that might have been scored for a string trio.

Whereas under those circumstances the reaction to each other's *kind* of sound is the determining factor, in the Adagio of Brahms's Sonata in F major the *length* of the piano sound will have to influence the choice of the tempo. The wide spacing of the melodic notes (see Ex. 6) on the piano will make the melody unintelligible when the playing is too slow or too pale. Of course, meanwhile the audience may have a wonderful time with some ringing pizzicato on the C-string and never know that there is a melody in the piano part. But such a result would be quite out of line with the approach I was advocating before, which was supposed to start with a study of *all* the elements of a score. The same consideration is also applicable to the development section of the first movement of this sonata. Though the cello's sextolets have to be clear and even, they also have to be fluent enough that the main voice, i.e., the augmentation of the movement's first motif on the piano, is understood (see Ex. 7).

Ex. 6

Ex. 7

When one melody is evenly divided between the two instruments and there is no question of wanting a break in the expression, the attempt at a close matching of sounds must be especially determined. An example may be the opening of Beethoven's Fourth Sonata, in C major (Ex.8), in which the cello intones the ascending half and the piano completes the arch. How very disappointing when the cellist ends his part of the statement, below which the piano has already entered softly, with an irrevocable calando, instead of handing it to his partner, and thus breaks the arch in two.

Ex. 8

These problems of matching timbre, speed, and structure to unify the two instruments are relatively easy to solve with a little imagination, compared to the discrepancies in articulation. For example, in the third theme of the opening Allegro of Beethoven's Sonata in A major, the piano's dotted rhythms (shown in Ex. 9), have an individual percussiveness even when played as legato as possible. The

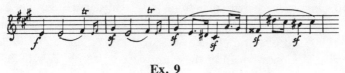

Ex. 9

cellist will have to strive consciously if he wants to achieve that same character or, for that matter, would like to have his articulation understood at all. That is not easy against the turbulence of the piano's sixteenth notes, an effect that may have to be achieved more by suggestion than by what one may be tempted to describe as "only playing forte as prescribed by the composer." I often feel that dynamic markings ought to be scrutinized as indicators of emotional intensity as much as for their denoting the degree of loudness. *Pianissimo* may mean, in addition to "very softly," also "hushed" or "felt deep within." (Schubert marks so many of his melodies *pp*, simply asking, it seems to me, for the utmost loveliness of expression.) One has to beware, therefore, of always attaching absolute meanings to dynamics indications. Absolute, as far as it is possible, should be the empathy with the composer's concept as intuition is reinforced by the intellectual absorption of the score. Absolute should be the clarity of a main voice. The notion of an absolute forte in the above example is quite unrealistic, however, especially since it is followed by a fortissimo. The discrepancy between Beethoven's and today's pianos furnishes further food for thought. How might the Alberti basses of the First Sonata for cello and piano have sounded on his piano? Or the repeated notes of the opening of Mendelssohn's Sonata in D major or of the C minor section in the exposition of Chopin's Cello Sonata on nineteenth-century instruments? These are the places where the ears have to be especially alert.

While we are at absolutes, may I caution young cellists that very fragile pianos and pianissimos will not project on the low strings in the company of keyboard figurations. And pizzicati played softly in a low register have even more difficulty being heard. An absolute piano is useless under these circumstances.

Let us return to Beethoven's Sonata in A major. In the legato scales of the second theme of the opening movement the problem is twofold. The piano has a difficult time, especially when the right hand plays octaves, in maintaining a legato that does not sound inferior to the string player's. The cellist has to contend with string-crossings and position changes that will in turn make him look like the pianist's poor cousin if they are not completely inaudible.

As a final example of a problematic legato match-up I would like to cite the opening of the finale of Brahms's Second Sonata (see Ex. 10). The phrasing slurs are very long here. On the piano they are realized easily, on the cello less so. The difficulty of maintaining a long legato line in spite of the unavoidable bow changes is compounded by the problem of executing the fingering smoothly. Often a very undesirable fragmentation of the theme is created—sometimes it sounds as though it were phrased in half measures, which is a real disaster—along with a heavy-handed tempo, which makes the later triplets sound elephantine. This would not seem to accord with Hugo Becker's recollection that Brahms liked to play this movement very fast.

Ex. 10

A superior ear and a fine technique can usually take care of the problems involving legato phrases. But the problems of matching abrupt sounds often remain as they never should in front of an audience: obviously difficult. The theme of the last movement of Brahms's Sonata in E minor is taken from the *Art of Fugue*. The first section of this movement, written as a triple fugue, ought to retain the clarity of a Bach fugue in spite of its Romantic development. This means that one ought to perceive each of the three themes clearly every time (that can be done by assigning to each theme a different part of the measure for its climactic stress); that the first theme and its inversion, played simultaneously, must both be intelligible; and that, in short, power must not vitiate transparency. There is a well-known story that Brahms replied to a cello partner who complained that he could not be heard that it was all for the better. I think we would rather stick close to the sensitive composer than to the rude pianist, an attitude I also like to adopt when listening to Shostakovich's own, very rough, recorded version of his beautiful Sonata for Cello and Piano.

In the Brahms fugato we have to match notes in length and strength, particularly in the triplets. There is not a chance in the world that the pianist can duplicate a cello sound produced on the string. A strong spiccato in the middle is still likely to be lacking in power and to be impure to boot. A broad arm stroke in the lower half, leaving the string on a flat arch (No. 3 below) seems to me to be the proper solution, matching a détaché finger action on the keyboard. I would recommend a similar stroke for the groups of three notes in the Scherzo of Brahms's Sonata in F major, but suggest for the opening groups of two bass notes a snappy finger action at the frog (No. 2 below), which propels the bow from the string into the air. I have a horror of hearing bows clattering down onto the string in this kind of situation.

Generally speaking, I think that abrupt sounds are the bane of string players and bother cellists perhaps more than violinists and violists because of the difficulty of response on the low strings. I am grateful that some strings currently on the market have alleviated this problem considerably.

But the difficulties really start with questions of performance practice. In the long and important period from the disappearance of the vertical staccato sign ('), as a mark of ending a note abruptly, to the introduction of compound signs like the dot-dash (÷), that is, from about middle Beethoven to the beginning of the twentieth century, the dot was virtually the only symbol to mark a separation of two adjoining sounds. It was left up to the player's sense of style to decide how short was short. Moreover, it was understood, especially in older music but applicable well into modern times, that even in the absence of a dot, notes not slurred implied a lift, the degree of which was regulated by nothing but taste. (I might cite as Brahmsian examples the coda of the first movement of the Clarinet Trio or the second theme of the finale of his Trio in C major. See Ex. 11.) That this is often not understood in our time results, for instance, in some mushy Mozart playing that not only robs melodies of their gracefulness but also clutters up performances with too many sustained sounds.

Ex. 11

In the cello literature we may point to the opening of the first Allegro of Beethoven's Second Sonata (Ex. 12). This movement abounds with dots but has none on the initial upbeat. If the cellist unthinkingly connects the upbeat smoothly to the downbeat, the answering phrase on the piano cannot help, because of the mechanics of the instrument, having a contrasting separation of sounds. A modern composer might have written ÷ for both instruments. Certainly this is not one of the places where, in the course of many different illuminations of the same theme, one might have fun stating them differently. The Beethoven theme shows just one of thousands of instances where a stringed instrument can sustain the sound completely during bow changes but should not do so.

Ex. 12

For whatever one is about to perform, I wish that the sound-concept would always be firmly established in the mind before one reaches into the toolbox and attempts to pull out the right tool. In the case of detached notes I would like to find this basic equipment in everybody's box: (1) a martelé stroke on the string, in all parts of the bow; (2) a stroke anywhere from the upper middle to the frog, starting from the string and winding up in the air; (3) an arm stroke slightly off the string in the lower half; (4) the bow thrown *onto* the string in the middle; (5) a rubbing stroke in the middle, propelled *from* the string. No. 1 suggests a total cessation of movement after every note. No. 2 may or may not involve a continuous arm motion, depending on the tempo, combined with sharply defined wrist snaps. These from-the-string strokes seem to me to be particularly worth cultivating as an intermediary between the obvious on-the-string and off-the-string bowings; Nos. 3 to 5 entail uninterrupted pendulum motions of the arm that establish contact with the string at the nadir of an arch. The greater or lesser (or, at great speed, even exclusive) use of wrist and fingers and the variability of the arch can determine the brushier or more percussive quality of the strokes. One ought to be able to make use of the five basic short strokes with great flexibility, selecting them in accordance with tempo and character. It would seem very restrictive to me and putting the cart before the horse to have to choose the tempo of a piece on the basis of the limited availability of short strokes. Each has its speed limit but should lead seamlessly into the next faster one.

This is not the place to talk of the innumerable compound strokes that may be developed from these basic ones. My main points with regard to their use are just these: the problem of resonant short strokes is a very real one; too often the solution chosen is not in conformity with the stylistic requirements of the passage at hand. Let there be clarity of purpose before the choice of the means, and let these means be manifold and finely honed.

Among the orchestral instruments, the strings are the most richly endowed group. True, they require the longest hours of practice and their superior specimens are, next to the organ, the most expensive musical instruments. But they possess the divine gift of being able to express anything a human heart ever dreamt about and to say it better than words ever will. In addition, they are unparalleled acrobats and magicians. The cello is an indispensable and extremely versatile member of this family. It has worked its way up to a position of technical respectability, and nobody has ever doubted its eloquence. The fate of its great potential rests today in the wonderfully gifted hands of many first-rate artists. The next generation promises to hold its banner high with unprecedented skill, with ingenuity and devotion.

May the musician writing about the "Cello Sounds of the Year Two Thousand" feel as sanguine about his beloved instrument as I do today.

Laurence Shapiro

The Violin Student in Search of Himself

INTRODUCTION

"How can I keep my bow from bouncing?"
"My vibrato gets tight all of a sudden."
"My stomach gets tied in knots."
"Suddenly I can't use the lower part of the bow."
"My legs start shaking."
"My heart beats so fast, I can't control anything."
"What can I do to control my nerves in performance?"

We have all heard these questions and complaints many times. We have all attempted, haltingly, to answer them. Yet we realize that there is an intrinsic irony in trying to solve performance problems for someone else when we have not yet solved them completely for ourselves.

In an attempt to define the causes of this universal, the practicing–performing dichotomy, I shall start with some broader thoughts, not directly related to violin playing or, in fact, to music at all, but pertaining to the preliminaries for any creative endeavor. In the second section of this chapter I shall examine, in a general way, the actual phenomenon of playing the violin; and in the third section I shall focus on specific technical or mental–technical problems. The closing section will deal with the lifeblood of creativity— communication.

We are the children of emptiness. In less than one hundred years all our comforters have been taken from us. "God is dead," cried Nietzsche. God, like Mark Twain, must have been surprised to hear this. But the death of God-in-Man as a viable life force has certainly become an overwhelming reality.

"Family is dead," we might also cry out. A seemingly entropic law pulls our nuclei apart with mindless, savage force, and sets us adrift in psychic space.

"Place is dead," we must also acknowledge. In the United States, particularly, we blow like Brownian tumbleweeds across the land, scattering seeds on often alien soils.

Finally and most devastatingly, we are alienated and even estranged from ourselves. In T. S. Eliot's tragically accurate visions of a half-century ago, we are "hollow men" inhabiting a waste land. Our heads are indeed "filled with straw." This existential malaise casts a powerful pall over our spiritual landscape and wafts easily into the soul of every individual who does not have the resources to fill himself with other than "straw."

The hollow man is totally outer-directed and totally reflecting, for like the lifeless Moon, his light does not come from within. He is out of touch with himself, does not know he is out of touch with himself, has no idea of who he is, and spends his time running in place like Alice, feeling either vaguely uneasy or quietly desperate through all his grey life.

Although the preceding paragraphs are certainly bleak and despairing, they describe only a partial reality, for they represent merely the thick priming of our contemporary canvas. How we overlay that prime coat, what colors and textures we paint on it, will determine whether or not we can ultimately transform it into something rich and meaningful.

SOME SUGGESTIONS FOR GETTING IN TOUCH WITH ONESELF
I. MACROCOSMIC APPROACHES:

Twenty-four hundred years have passed since Socrates summarized his restless, ultimately fatal search with two words, "Know thyself." No one before or since has dug a deeper philosophical foundation, though amazing structures have certainly been built upon it. Yet this terse motto, which is at the root of every human problem, is little practiced and less understood.

Granted, to "know thyself" is a difficult task—no doubt, the *most* difficult one. Granted, it is unquestionably a lifelong task. Granted, too, that the pursuit is a frustrating one, that the moments of success are rare and fleeting, but the instant of *self-discovery* is so transcendent, beautiful, and charged with meaning that we come to realize that the most difficult task is also the only task worthy of the name.

In every sentient human being there exists an essential dichotomy, a primitive destructive force or being, bending all its energies toward frustrating the part of the self that is attempting to succeed. It does not matter whether we think of it as Dr. Doolittle's Pushmi-Pullyu, as the Satan of the fundamentalist Christian, as the Parent in the Child of Transactional Analysis, as the Engram of the Scientologist, or as the guilt trip of the Freudian analyst. The fact remains that we have all been victimized by it and frustrated in our efforts to reach the highest possible levels of creativity and happiness.

Man is a complex creature, indeed, truly the "ghost in the machine." To know himself he must first know the machine intimately and treat it with great deference, for that is the only way he can come to know the elusive "ghost"—himself.

The Violinist as Athlete

On the first level is the basic well-being of the machine—the body. Playing the violin is a highly demanding physical endeavor, and like an athlete, the violinist must constantly be "in training." The endurance required of the large muscles and the exquisite precision asked of the small muscles demand that we give utmost respect to the care and feeding of the body. The commonplaces of health must be scrupulously observed. I recommend that the violinist eat healthfully, take vitamins, get plenty of rest, and exercise regularly. One must not defile the body and the senses with uppers, downers, or sidewaysers. Drugs, alcohol and sugar in excessive amounts, and smoking serve no constructive purpose.

The practice of Yoga has been going on for about six thousand years. The word itself means "union." There are many different kinds of Yoga, each a separate way of life, though each can be practiced in conjunction with every other. Yoga does not claim to be a religion, though on its most mystical levels the union is one with

God. The practice of simple Hatha Yoga—Yoga exercises—is a wonderful companion for any spiritual or religious pursuit, since it occupies itself with union on the first level—the level of this discussion, union with self.

On a totally physical level, Yoga exercises represent a fine fulfillment of the "violinist as athlete" concept. All Yoga positions, even the most elementary, are designed for two purposes: to stretch a portion of the body, and to remove tension. Surely limberness and relaxation are the two most sought-after physical goals of the violinist; the acquiring of these qualities alone would make the investment of fifteen or twenty minutes each morning very worthwhile.

When Yoga breathing is added to the practicing of the Asanahs (positions), a deeper level is reached. The concept of drawing in Prahna (life force) from the air while inhaling, and of expelling impurities and tensions when exhaling, is a powerful piece of imagery. The physiological benefits of deep, slow Yogic breathing[1]— enrichment of the blood, greater stretch, and increased heart and lung capacity—combine with the concept described above to produce a blissful feeling of well-being and inner peace that can linger for hours.

Since breathing is synonymous with life itself, this deep, reflective use of breathing should be used throughout the day, not only in conjunction with the Asanahs. It is an invaluable aid to centering oneself before and during performance—of music or of any other demanding task.[2]

An Actor Prepares

The theories of Konstantin Stanislavski and their realization by the Moscow Art Theatre represent the finest systematic transformation, from self-examination into art, in existence. Acting and musical performance are closely related. They are both re-creative arts, they both occur in time as well as space, and they both have the potential for reaching the most profound depths of human consciousness and

1. Filling and emptying the entire vessel of the self, from below the diaphragm.
2. Other practices that may produce similar results for some people include Tai Chi, karate, Transcendental Meditation, and chanting. The Alexander Technique is also somewhat related, in that it seeks to align the spine, which is the seat of youth and the avenue of messages to the brain.

the most transcendent and ecstatic moments of human experience. We musicians would be much poorer, indeed, if we failed to recognize the elements they have in common.

Stanislavski's "Method" exercises will produce a heightened awareness of one's body, an increased ability to concentrate and to *live in the moment,* and a profound knowledge of and intimacy with aspects of oneself of which one was not previously aware. Many people take acting classes simply to become freer physically and emotionally. They find acting much less expensive and much more effective than analysis. It seems to me almost imperative that musicians read Stanislavski and practice his exercises; they might also be well advised to take acting classes.

When I was a young college student, I came across a modest little book that changed my life, *Zen in the Art of Archery* by Eugen Herrigel.[3] Its important message is the essential unity of man with his "thing," whether it be archery, flower arranging, inkbrush painting, or playing the violin. For the archer the moment comes when he, the bow, the arrow, the target, and the space between them become one. For the musician, after long contemplation of this mystical union, the moment can come when he, the instrument, the music, the sound, and the audience become one. I frequently find myself saying to a student, "You and your instrument must together become an instrument, a vehicle through which the music passes, like light through a stained-glass window."[4]

II. "DOIN' WHAT COMES NATURALLY"

I have had the good fortune to know and to study with a number of fine musicians. One of the greatest, a man who has profoundly influenced me, is Raphael Bronstein. Bronstein speaks about music and violin playing in almost metaphysical terms, in paradoxical aphorisms. All of them, however, derive from one basic insight: *The*

3. New York: Pantheon, 1953. After reading and re-reading the book over a period of several years, I learned that Herrigel had subsequently become a Nazi. Although this was most discouraging news to me personally, I decided not to let this side of Herrigel turn me away from what had been good, beautiful, and true in him.

4. In the analogy the glass is not clear because just as stained glass enriches light, so can the player's personality enrich the music, if he is in total inner harmony with it.

same is not the same! In this section I shall discuss some of the manifestations of this essential paradox, first in the physical realm and then in the aural one.

The Wrongness of What Comes Naturally: The Body

What can it mean, "The same is not the same"? It means that although a person perceives himself as doing one thing, in fact something quite different is really happening. Through an understanding of this principle and its application, many playing problems can be overcome.

There is one other physical fact that we recognize: *The human body is not designed for playing the violin!* It is much better designed for playing the cello, or the piano, or the clarinet, or the dombeg, or tennis. Once we accept this unfortunate truth, it is possible to come to terms with the body and ultimately create for it an illusion of naturalness.

With knowledge of these two correlative principles—Bronstein's paradox and the unsuitableness of the human body—half the battle is won, and we may, with intelligence and foresight, solve the physical problems involved.

Bow direction is perhaps the most widely recognized example of "The same is not the same." It is well known that if the right arm travels "straight"—that is, in a way that feels "natural"—then the bow travels crookedly, the tip starting (on down-bow) behind the ear and ending over the fingerboard. The solution to this paradox is obvious: Cause the hand to travel a crooked path and the bow will travel straight.

I must at this point add a cautionary note: It is generally a *quite subtle* modification that must be made. The precise modification depends, of course, on the length of the player's arm and on the position of the instrument. Adjusting the position of the instrument can, in fact, have a dramatically beneficial effect on bow direction. Many students, however, employ the corrective forward pumping motion both too soon and too much, to the point where the tip of the bow is angled toward the bridge; in this position the more pressure that is applied the harsher and more choked the tone will be.

From this simple example it may be seen that paradox-solving is a very tricky business. Each student must see himself as an individual and a unique physical person, and must be treated as such by his teacher.

Place your left hand on the nearest flat surface, palm down, in a totally relaxed position. You will immediately see why everyone, from beginners to professionals, has difficulty playing well in tune. So, with respect to intonation also, the body is not designed for playing the violin. The hand is innocent of such refinements as half-steps and whole-steps. The ring finger in particular lies impotent, lacking the independence of the others and located too far from the middle finger for a decent half-step and much too close for a whole-step. The fourth finger is much shorter that the others and emerges from the hand at the "wrong" angle. When one adds to these difficulties the fact that the interval size shrinks as one ascends, and the fact that new variables are introduced on each string, it is no wonder that perfect intonation is the rarest musical flower of all.

Yet there is a simple principle that will produce fine, resonant intonation in most contexts. Like all simple principles it is easier said than done. But if the student can train his mind to observe it scrupulously, his hand will respond with dramatically improved intonation. The principle is: *large whole-step relationships and small half-step relationships*. The word "relationships" includes notes played on adjacent strings. The half-step relationships are therefore half-steps, tritones, and minor sixths; the whole-step relationships are whole-steps, perfect fourths, and major sixths.

Once in a studio class, when I was going on at some length about the importance of developing extensions between all combinations of fingers, a student challenged me with, "Why do we have to practice extensions, anyway?" I thought a moment and suddenly knew the answer. "So that we can play in tune in first position," I answered her.

As the Yogis say, "The body seeks comfort." That is the body's mistake, perhaps the greatest example of the wrongness of "doin' what comes naturally." As the auto mechanic on a television commercial says, "You can pay me now [for an oil filter] or you can pay me later [for a major engine repair]." Analogously, what we call "comfort" in youth is really laziness, which we "pay for later" with stiffness in middle and old age. I would much prefer to "pay now" with a little daily "discomfort" (Yoga exercises) in order to keep the spine and limbs young and supple throughout a long life.

Similarly, the hand seeks comfort. Like a violin string, it seeks to go back where it came from. That is why it must be stretched out every day, gently but firmly. Only then can it reasonably be called upon to produce perfect intonation in the most difficult place—in first position.

Now it is only fair to point out that the violin is not made for playing the body! As one crosses the strings from E to G one realizes again that "The same is not the same." With the same bow pressure the volume diminishes, for the A-string is not as brilliant as the E, the D is much duller than the A, and the G, though as loud or louder than the D, is nevertheless much darker in color. In addition there is the illusion problem: The listener automatically perceives a descending line as getting softer, even if it doesn't, so that double compensation must often be made.

In descending scalewise motion there is yet another problem: The same finger pressure on a less-resonant finger (4 after 1, or 3 after 0) will itself cause a considerable rupture in the line. Not only the bow must compensate, but the finger as well.

These are only two of the many reasons for practicing scales. Ultimately we find they contain almost all the problems to be encountered in the repertoire.

Before leaving this section I would like to make a final suggestion. The first rule of beautiful tone production is: *The comfort of the bow arm is of paramount importance*. Since the arm is not comfortable either scraping alongside the body or hoisted up above the shoulder, it is strongly suggested that the student develop the technique of "playing the bow with the violin"—bringing the extreme strings (G and E) close to the bow. The platform of the violin can easily be flattened or tilted with a subtle motion of the back and/or shoulder, thus radically diminishing the vertical distance the bow arm must travel.[5]

5. This concept was first suggested to me by the brilliant pedagogue Harold Berkley, whose book *The Modern Technique of Violin Bowing* (New York: G.

The Rightness of What Comes Naturally: The Sound

Last year several of my students banded together and had a T shirt made for me. I was very touched by the gesture, and was particularly pleased by what they had selected, for it is certainly one of the most important tenets of my teaching. On the front is printed:

PLAY OFF YOUR SOUND

SHAPIROISM NUMBER 1001

Play off your sound. The words themselves have a lovely ring, as does their application. But what, exactly, does this slogan mean?

Sound is one of the most basic, primitive, and pervasive of all realities. The entire universe and everything in it are in a constant and eternal state of vibration—a kind of cosmic hum. Even the Bible agrees, for "In the beginning was the word." (Perhaps that is why during rare ecstatic moments—often while alone—one feels something close to a religious experience, binding him to the sound, sound that he is both producing and being immersed in.)

Sound is an overwhelming reality, a constant stream of majestic power waiting to be tapped, waiting to envelop the player in himself. *But most players never hear themselves!* That is not a glib statement tossed out for its shock value; it is a fact.

While you are playing, have someone turn off the light suddenly. Continue playing and listen. What you hear will probably amaze you. For the first time you will have no way to throw up barriers between yourself and the sound. With the too-powerful sense of sight removed, you will no longer be able to worry about position, bow direction, elbows, thumbs, feet, sheet music, or any other visual distractions. You will know only the black velvet embracing you and the sound. You will hear an immediate and marked improvement in beauty of tone, sustaining of tone, vibrato, intonation, and phrasing.

Now it becomes clear that there are really two quite polarized approaches to violin playing. The first is directed by the left side of the brain, which processes information serially and linearly and is highly rational. It trains the body, bit by bit, to do everything

Schirmer, 1941) is perhaps the finest and most gracefully written exposition on the subject.

necessary to produce a beautiful, appropriate, and in-tune sound. It works from the body to the sound.

The second approach is directed by the right side of the brain, which is intuitive, primitive, and non-rational. It consists of imagining the sound first, playing off that image, and allowing the body to find the means to reproduce that sound. It works from the sound to the body.

Practice in the dark. If you can't make the room dark during the day, close your eyes. Let your senses overlap, so that in a synesthetic raptus you suddenly feel you are *touching the sound* with your fingertips. Then listen.

III. Microcosmic Approaches:
Some Suggestions for Getting in Touch with One's
Body–Mind and Its Instrumental Extension

Earlier I suggested the image of the violinist and his instrument together becoming an instrument. But this cannot happen until certain specific awarenesses have been programmed in the brain. The reader may immediately assume that this is fancy language for plain old practicing. Such is not the case, for nonspecific, inattentive, lackadaisical, or low-energy practicing will yield relatively little return for one's time. Practicing which is not existential—that is, which is not grounded in the moment—is of little enduring value. If there is such a thing as a shortcut, it is only in practicing very specifically, with total moment-to-moment concentration, with great sensory awareness, and with knowledge of the ways in which the mind and the body learn best.

Music minus One

The great Brazilian cellist Aldo Parisot once said jokingly that someone should invent a cutaway cello, similar to a cutaway guitar, so that the body of the instrument would not hinder shifting. Yet Parisot deals with an instrument that is fairly comfortable to play. It is firmly rooted in the floor, and one need not fear dropping it.

But what of the poor violinist? What is his floor? Obviously it is his own body, particularly his upper chest and his head. Only when the instrument is supported firmly, without the aid of the hand, can one comfortably proceed to more complex matters, such as shifting. A shoulder pad of some kind may definitely be employed, for the "support system" must be established with a minimum of back-muscle involvement. ("Chest pad" would be a much more accurate and useful description of this object.)

A simple way to encourage the mind to focus on this firm platform, or "support system," is to remove the left thumb from the instrument! You will immediately be forced to support the instrument with your body and a heavy head. With the thumb removed temporarily, many problems can be alleviated: Clenching the instrument is no longer possible, shifting becomes fluid and all jerks are eliminated, and a much more specific knowledge of the fingerboard is gained. And with the reluctant thumb gone, the elbow comes around naturally when necessary, eliminating the barrier to shifting posed by the body of the instrument.

Most important of all, you become aware of the true source of support for the instrument and learn how that support can give freedom to the hand. Ten of fifteen minutes daily should be devoted to practicing without using the thumb.

The Ice Cream Scoop

If I had to describe in a brief phrase the essential characteristics of a fine position—which was beautiful, utile, and strong—I would say, *straight forearms and round hands*. Actually the achievement of one often suffices to produce the other, though both should be pursued as worthy goals.

To achieve straight forearms (without bent wrists), I suggest spending several minutes daily before a mirror observing the improvements brought about by two exercises: To bring the left hand into line, hold the thumb fairly high and straight up. To solve the bent-wrist problem of the right hand, practice an athletic follow-through by the forearm on up-bow, so that the back of the wrist ends up somewhere near the nose.

Concerning round hands, the problem is not so easily disposed of, for the hands must not only be round but also be strong in the round shape. The naturalness of the round hand shape can be demonstrated by making fists, relaxing them, and sticking a violin into one and a bow into the other. But we do not play the violin with our fists, and the round strength must be developed in the individual fingers of both hands.

People crush paper, squeeze handballs, and do bizarre things with rubber bands in an effort to gain the needed strength. But these devices build only a generalized power in the hands, suitable perhaps for protecting oneself from bone-crushing well-wishers in the greenroom, but not for such tasks as trilling thirds or playing pianissimo string skips at the frog.

I have found only one device that builds round strength. It can be bought at the supermarket for a dollar, comes in plastic or metal in a variety of attractive colors, and can even be used for festive occasions. It is the ice cream scoop, a modest gadget perfectly designed for developing round strength in the third and fourth fingers of each hand. Oppose the third and fourth fingers, individually or together, with the thumb; then squeeze. Remember to keep the fingers round. It is also useful to carry one's case with these two fingers, lifting it up and down while walking. Alternate hands frequently to avoid strain.

The Development of Extensions

A ballet dancer, gymnast, or football player would never dream of performing without a long and carefully graded limbering and stretching of the body. Yet we think nothing of picking up the violin and subjecting the hand to violent abuse, forcing it to stretch when it is not ready. Furthermore, almost all methods dealing with extending the hand go about it backwards, with possibly severe consequences, by starting low and ending high. In fact, they unwisely start in first position, where the intervals are the widest, and on the lowest string, where the stretch demands are even more dangerous. Since extensions are a fact of a violinist's life, and since playing in tune in first position is a worthy goal of such a life, extensions must be developed, of course. But that process must be done gently, gradually, and with common sense. I have formulated a set of simple exercises that safely develop a considerable extending ability and that have the added benefit of sharpening the ear.

Select a pair of fingers—let us say, 3 and 4—and work with a double-stop that would be ludicrously large in first position—in this case a major seventh. Work only on the A- and E-strings, where the extensions are the smallest. Don't even attempt to play the interval in first position but go immediately to the corresponding pitches one octave above first position. You will be pleasantly surprised to find that the interval is quite feasible up there. By "inch-worming" down slowly from this position:

M7—m7	M7—m7	M7—m7	M7—m7, etc.
D–C♯—D–C	C♯–C—C♯–B	C–B—C–B♭	B–B♭—B–A

you will soon develop a fine feeling of rubbery strength between these two fingers. Repeat each interval at least once, so that the descent will be as slow as possible.

Whenever you practice extensions, vibrate continuously; if you can vibrate, you are not dangerously extended. Do not descend to the point of actual pain. Tomorrow is another day, and perhaps you will go one half-step farther then. Someday you might even get all the way down to first position. If the M7—m7 is too large for you initially, begin with one half-step smaller, with m7—M6. The principle remains the same, and you will gain the same facility. The other intervals I use are:

Finger Pair	Interval
2–3	M7—m7
1–2	M9—m9
2–4	M9—m9
1–3	m10—M9
1–4	A11—P11

Give each vibrating interval two long, sustained bow strokes, for the descent must be very gradual if you are to realize the full benefits of the exercise and avoid strain. In addition, it is important to develop the extension from the thumb, which is invaluable in high positions.

Mastering Passages by Redirecting the Mind

Music occurs in time. One note leads to another in an orderly, linear sequence. Therefore, the preliminary procedure toward ultimate mastery must be performed on this most primitive level, that of connecting one note to the next. I shall use the Presto from Bach's Sonata in G minor for the examples. Ex. 1 presents the first step, which should be played beginning both down- and up-bow.

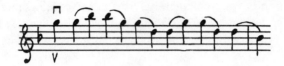

Ex. 1

The second procedure involves a diversion in the form of speed, but speed only in the right hand. Play the same passage giving each note four rapid spiccato (or détaché) strokes (as in Ex. 2). This playing will accomplish a variety of goals: (1) The torpid fingers will speak with springs, since the correct moment for lifting or dropping has suddenly become a very brief one. (2) You begin to locate the two elements that make the passage problematical—shifts and string-crossings (or skips). (3) While the mind is diverted to the precision requirements of the bow, the left hand continues to learn the notes—but at a very slow melodic speed.

Ex. 2

Next, repeat the passage in precisely the same fashion but starting up-bow. You will instantly feel much less in control, and you will have to concentrate even more on precise coordination. You will be learning to an even greater degree the location of string-crossings and shifts. And the left hand will continue, in its unhurried pace, to learn the notes.

The next step is to increase the melodic speed gradually. First increase it by 33 percent by reducing the number of strokes per note from four to three; then increase it another 50 percent by going from three strokes to two. Play each reduction beginning down-bow and then up-bow. At each step the concentration demands for coordination of the bow become greater. And off in a mental corner, the fingers keep on learning the notes.

The third procedure introduces the element of speed into the left hand, but in a way that the brain can deal with—on every other note, using dotted rhythms. First the passage is treated with a dotted eighth–sixteenth pattern, as in Ex. 3; then with a Hungarian style sixteenth–dotted eighth pattern, shown in Ex. 4.

Ex. 3

Ex. 4

Examine this bowing, it is *not* to be played like that in Ex. 5, which cannot be cleanly articulated. Remember to begin each treatment both down- and up-bow.

Ex. 5

Finally you are ready for the fourth procedure—building up the continuous speed of the passage with a metronome. My method is to select the tempo I wish to reach, go one marking beyond it, and count back nine markings. I then play it once at that very slow speed, twice at the next, three times at the next, and so on, until ultimately I play it ten times at one marking beyond the ideal tempo.[6]

This sequence involves a minimum of 67 playings of a given passage. That may seem terribly time-consuming, but it is the closest thing to a shortcut we have in our craft. A player may pirouette through a passage ten thousand times, but if he is too fast, sloppy, or inattentive (all of which he probably will be), he will never truly know it. But if he uses the method outlined above, he will possess it permanently.

Memorization

The most destructive phrase among musicians must be "Let's take it from the top." The "top" is generally polished until it gleams, but rare is the performance that radiates such a golden sheen throughout. Many a soloist, quartet, or orchestra staggers headlong from the brilliant clearing of the "top" into an unfamiliar forest of form and content.

"Backwards chaining" is one of the few psychological theories that have been demonstrated to be effective in practice. As an aid to both sophisticated learning and memory, it is unsurpassed. Nothing else can give the player such a feeling of security and comfort, for unlike the "take-it-from-the-topper," the "backwards chainer" is going into ever *more* familiar territory.

Like the procedures described in the last section, all that is required is patience and concentration. The technique is ridiculously simple: Begin by playing the last measure; then play the last two measures; follow this, not surprisingly, with a playing of the last three measures, etc. (Do not attempt to do an entire movement in this way, unless you have several days at your disposal. Work with the last section, then the next to last section, etc.) Again, it may be pointed out that this arduous, time-consuming procedure is, in fact, a kind of shortcut, for once you learn and memorize the piece in this way, it is yours for life.

6. Do not overlook the possibility of working down through the metronome speeds to master problems of bow distribution in slow movements. Use the same procedure, but in reverse.

A Helping Hand

Mr. Bronstein used to say, "The hands must be like acrobats: They work in complete harmony, yet each is perfectly independent." I suspect that Mr. Bronstein was describing a Platonic ideal to be sought after, not a reality. Obviously there are many times when the hands must act in opposition (e.g., in a rapid, slurred passage to be played pianissimo, the fingers of the left hand will speak like machine-gun bullets, while the right hand floats across the string, like cotton candy).

But our two halves are rather tightly strung together, and each has enormous sympathy for the other. In many cases a problem in one hand can be minimized or eliminated by sympathetic behavior in the other. I shall cite only two examples, though many more could be called forth.

Let us say, for the first case, that a rapid slurred passage with a sudden ascending shift in the middle is causing problems. You play the passage over and over, but you continue to have great difficulty around the shift. The notes before and after it remain jerky, fuzzy, and out of tune. With a sudden increase of the bow speed in the vicinity of the shift, the jerkiness in the left hand will disappear, the shift will reach far enough, and the notes that follow will be clear and in tune.

In the second case a note must be sustained powerfully and dramatically. You cannot prevent yourself from using excessive bow speed, paradoxically thwarting the very goals you set out to achieve. But if you employ an intense vibrato after the initial attack, the bow will instantly stick to the string like glue, and you will achieve the necessary sustaining.

These two examples involve real problems in one hand that can be solved by sympathetic behavior in the other. But there is another large category of apparent problems, in which the problem actually does reside in the other hand. How often has a student crunched the bow with excessive pressure, in an attempt to produce a loud clear tone, when in fact the problem is really insufficient finger pressure in the left hand! How often has a slide to a harmonic failed to arrive because the bow is no longer on the string!

If a technical problem appears to be troubling you in one hand, try looking at the other before assigning culpability.

Isolation

For Plato the so-called free man was actually a total slave—to his passions, appetites, and illusions. The *truly* free man was highly self-disciplined, self-denying, and self-knowing. This paradox is as urgent a messenger of truth today as it was for Plato. It is, in fact, largely through paradox that we find true meaning in our lives.

Our goal as musicians is to create a community of one, a many-faceted system that functions in perfect inner harmony. In the studio, through the use of an organic vehicle such as "playing off your sound," it may well come into being. Even in performance the magic might sometimes happen.

But the true artist is first a craftsman. Like Stanislavski's actor he "prepares," "builds his character," does his Method exercises. Only then does he go on stage—secure in the knowledge that he has done all he can to prepare himself—and act. And sometimes he is touched by a divine spark, and he becomes the character.

Here is the paradox: *Self-union can only be achieved by building each separate part in isolation.* It cannot be willed into being; the more you try to force it to happen, the deeper it will hide. Each element must be worked on as separately as is possible.

That would seem to be a joyless endeavor, but for a wonderful phenomenon: As one aspect of playing is improved, it infects the others, so that the process of creating a union with oneself, of developing a harmonious whole system, is constantly being accelerated.

If you are working on intonation, don't worry about bow direction; if tonal clarity, with each finger in the center of its pad, is your goal, don't concern yourself with bow distribution; if a sustained ribbon of sound from frog to tip is your target, don't fret about vibrato. Practice in isolation; the union will take care of itself. Both extremes must be included in daily practice, however: Each day should close with one or two full-energy performance run-throughs, so that you do not get squeezed down into a tiny, inhibiting, analytical box.

Why practice so diligently, anyway? In this era of moral relativism and so-called situational ethics, it seems almost inappropriate to bring such integrity to one's work. The answer can only come from within the self.

For Maimonides it was simple: Each man has inside him a moral imperative toward perfection.

For St. Thomas Aquinas it was also obvious: We are all vessels —of different sizes, to be sure—but vessels nonetheless, which must be filled.

For Pablo Casals the answer was perhaps most eloquent, and certainly most relevant to us. After he had passed his ninetieth birthday he was asked, "Don Pablo, you have been acknowledged as the world's greatest cellist for well over sixty years now; why do you continue to practice three hours every day?"

The little man replied, "Because I feel I am making progress."

IV. COMMUNICATION

So far this chapter has concentrated on ways to achieve communication with oneself. But we live among people, and now it is time to consider ways of reaching out to others.

Student–Teacher

To the student: You are a member of the questioning generation. You have every right to be cynical, critical, and discouraged by much of the world around you. But when you put yourself in the hands of a violin teacher, you must suspend all judgmental attitudes. The ancient craftsman relationship of master and apprentice must be embraced, as you give yourself wholeheartedly and completely to the ideas of your teacher. To do otherwise is only to steal from yourself. Like an uncritical sponge, you must soak up every drop of technical insight and musical wisdom. Later on, when you have finished this part of your studies, you may look back with more discrimination and carefully discard what is not right for you.

To the teacher: Let us assume that the student has fulfilled his part of the bargain: He has brought to the relationship sufficient intelligence, acceptable tools, a receptive attitude, and good will. The responsibility is now yours: You must find the means to communicate with him.

Pedagogy is composed of one part speechcraft and nine parts repetition. You must be artful enough to find the language spoken by your student and his body, and then you must be willing to repeat yourself, ad nauseam, until you have gotten through to him.

The repetition part is clear enough—but what of the linguistic one? You must be able and willing to express the same concept many different ways, until one rings a bell with a particular student, and he is able to achieve the specific goal you are both striving for.

In the area of student–teacher communication then, given an atmosphere of goodwill, it may be said that there are no failures on the part of the student, only those of the teacher—and none of us is immune to such a failure occasionally.

Composer–Performer

Gustav Mahler was the greatest conductor of his time, particularly for the operas of Wagner. He drove himself and his orchestra pitilessly in his striving for excellence. The musicians resented this man, who treated them simply as extensions of himself—a self for whom he had no consideration—in his reaching out for perfection. But his performances were memorable, for he sought, in the words of Bruno Walter, "to re-create the moment of creation." What an awesome assignment, and yet how rich the rewards for even partial success!

Creative artists are touched by the hand of Plato's "divine madness." Thus they live on a much deeper level of human consciousness than do most people. Their moments of ecstasy are transcendent, their moments of despair unbearably desolate. The blueprint they entrust to us is endowed with these larger-than-life qualities.

We must immerse ourselves in the composer, in his time, in his life. We must seek to crawl inside him, to become him. We must fall in love with the soul mirrored in his music. With perfect fidelity to the blueprint, we must seek, in every way possible, to divine his intentions—to "re-create the moment of creation." That is our mission as performers. To the extent that we succeed, our lives and the lives of our listeners are deepened, ennobled, and enriched forever.

Performer–Audience

The composer sets down the symbols; the performer actualizes them; but only when the audience receives them is the experience completed, only then is the longing of the blueprint fulfilled. Yet the tragic irony of the performer's life is that the presence of the audience makes him "nervous" and prevents him from delivering the message of beauty—a message he knows so well in the practice room.

The nimble mind must be stilled. Time must stop. All outer-directed strands of the self must be recalled, and the player must achieve a state of exclusive communion with himself. This is the great paradox of music: *The only way to communicate with an audience is to withdraw from it entirely.*

Nerves cannot be banished with an effort of will, but they can be crowded out of the consciousness so completely that their message never reaches the brain, and therefore cannot be transferred to any part of the body. In the prototype for this technique, the Lamaze method of natural childbirth, pain is not banished, but it is so completely crowded out of the consciousness by breathing exercises and focusing of the eyes, that its message never reaches the brain.[7]

In filling the brain so completely an existential dimension enters, for when the self is that firmly centered, there is no room for the twin time-devils—Past and Future. One is totally grounded in the moment.[8]

David Oistrakh was once asked whether everything he did on stage was planned. "Every whisper," was the answer. Every bow-speed pattern, movement of the legs, vibrato pattern, breath, slide-speed pattern was completely choreographed in advance. Completely filling his mind with moment-to-moment technical assignments, Oistrakh was an outstanding exemplar of this approach.

Richard Burton's memorable *Hamlet* of about twelve years ago, which was generated entirely by vocal–technical means—pitch, volume, and duration—is another remarkable example. No building of the character was employed, no emotional memory was engaged in, yet audiences were consistently moved by Burton's performance.

The great contemporary pedagogue Dorothy Delay is primarily an exponent of Technical Programming. The numerous outstanding young artists she has produced are a living testimony to the efficacy of this approach.

Taken together, these three examples make clear the often illusory

7. Irwin Chabon, *Awake and Aware* (New York: Delacorte, 1969).
8. The model for the achievement of this degree of temporal immediacy is *Inner Tennis* by W. Timothy Gallwey (New York: Random House, 1976).

nature of a great performance. For with this approach it matters not what emotions or personal fulfillment the performer feels (or does not feel). The only thing that matters is how the audience is affected.

There exists in each of us a primitive turbulence, a mass of often undefined emotions, which we spend much of our psychic energy in repressing. The Method seeks to free that trapped power and make constructive use of it by channeling it into performance. The fascinating thing about this approach is that the emotion tapped need not correspond to the emotion called for in a given musical movement or dramatic scene! All that is needed is to release some emotion—any emotion—whichever one seems to be the essential you at the moment. It can be anger, hatred, or even frustration. If you can develop the courage to face it and then tap into it, you and your audience are in store for a powerful, exhausting experience.

The only drawback to this approach is that it is so terribly draining. On a long concert tour or an extended theatrical run, it is not practical or safe. That is why Peter Brooke's Broadway production of *Marat/Sade* had several alternating casts, so that the actors could recover from the exhausting experience of spilling their emotional guts on stage every night. Even so, a number of them suffered nervous collapses during and after the long run of the play. Your emotional store is more powerful than you imagine. Tap into it with great care.

When my brothers were little boys and the time came to go to bed, my father would say to them, "Kiss your father as though you love him." Of course, they proceeded to embrace him with great warmth, for the gentle humor of the suggestion very effectively focused their feelings. The use of the fantasy phrase "as though" (you love him) brought home to them that, in fact, they did.

Often I say to my students, "Play the music as though it were beautiful." They chuckle at the irony of the phrase, but suddenly realize that they have been figuratively giving the music only a perfunctory peck on the cheek—earnestly executing the notes instead of basking in their beauty, playing on the violin instead of in the violin, playing at the music instead of merging with it.

I believe that artists who make us smile and feel warm inside—

artists like Fritz Kreisler, Joseph Szigeti, and Josef Gingold—are inspired by the pure love of the music. Their primary motivating force is to play it "as though it were beautiful."

Filling the brain with this lovely, humanistic phrase is such a simplistic-sounding way of centering the self that many students have a difficult time taking it seriously. Yet for me it is the most effective path to creative solipsism. By surrendering myself totally to the realization that the music I am playing is really very beautiful, I find myself falling in love with it anew each moment. Then I can most easily reach that rare state where music, sound, instrument, and I become one—and that One is all that exists.

Abraham Skernick

Water Seeks Its Own Level

I remember learning in General Science in elementary school that "water seeks its own level." I can still visualize the experimental equipment: a large glass chamber, consisting of many turrets of different heights and varying widths—some rectangular, some cylindrical—all open at the top and all sharing the same large base. When water was poured into one of the "stacks" it fell directly into the base and gradually rose evenly and to the same level in all the stacks. It didn't seem to matter how wide or narrow they were. The water rose to the same level in each of them as long as it was being poured. I was convinced. Water certainly did seek its own level.

Years later, in a college physics laboratory, I saw the same kind of experiment performed again. But this time the equipment was slightly different. Some of the stacks were tall and very thin, with tiny diameters. The water rose higher in those tubes than it did in the vessels of greater diameter. The narrower the tube, the higher the level! This phenomenon was explained as "capillary attraction." The water tended to adhere to the walls of the various stacks. Indeed, it adhered to all the walls. You could see that the liquid "sloped upward" toward all the walls, even in the larger vessels. Some of the vessels were so narrow that they didn't have enough of a central area where the water could "sit" at its basic level, so the level itself appeared to be higher.

Did the second experiment disprove the first? Of course not! Water *does* seek its own level. Capillary attraction is a refinement of the original truth, a greater insight into the truth.

We may encounter many examples of this sort of thing in our learning experiences. At first, we learn basic fundamentals. Later

118

we discover refinements, some of which may seem to contradict the fundamentals. If we continue to experiment, and apply logic and wisdom, we may add to our fund of knowledge and to a deeper understanding of the fundamentals.

As a teacher of advanced viola students, I find that much of my time is spent in explaining and demonstrating refinements of what they were previously taught. I occasionally find that I have to teach the opposite of what was originally taught by their first teachers. But most of the time, when I tell a student to do something differently, I am teaching a refinement. I am explaining the capillary attraction that leads to a better understanding of the original water-level concept.

One of the first things learned by all beginners on the violin or viola is to "keep that elbow under" the instrument. This is absolutely necessary, of course, but it seems so unnatural at first, and completely different from anything the student has ever done with his left arm. There is nothing more difficult and uncomfortable, at first, than twisting the arm into that awkward contortion that gets the left elbow directly below the fiddle—and nothing more annoying and irritating than the constant nagging to "keep it there." I have the greatest sympathy for all such beginners. What they are asked to do with the left arm is not merely unnatural; it is actually painful! I'm sure that thousands of beginners give up after a few weeks of this torture and that is why there are so many pianists and guitar players—and cellists.

What is surprising to me is that there *are* so many violinists and violists (the "chin-strings" as George Szell used to call them). And what is amazing to me is that so many of them are playing their instruments "the hard way," with the left arm contorted much more than is necessary. Not only students but many professionals as well go through life with their left arms twisted far beyond what is required by their fingers. I have seen fiddlers (and that includes violists) who have their left arms so far "under" that they would be able to play their instruments with the scrolls pointing straight ahead of them if that were desirable. Instead, they play with a tremendous bend of the left wrist in order to be able to place their fingers on the strings where the instrument is actually positioned. They play virtually everything with the same rigid left-arm position. The arm is under far enough to enable them to play on the C-string with a rich, mellow tone. As they go across the strings, the sound gets drier and thinner, and when they play on the lower A-string, the sound is nasal and metallic and the vibrato is practically nonexistent. As they go from the lowest string to the highest, with the left arm unyielding, the fingers become more arched, until they are playing on the very tips, with the fingers almost tightly clenched on the highest string.

Of course, the pain is no longer present, or maybe it still hurts but they have become used to it. In any case, the tension must be tremendous, and tension is the enemy of the string player. It affects the sound, the shifting technique, the ability to adjust pitch, and the stamina and general efficiency of the left hand. There is nothing worse for the technique than the exaggeration of something that is not natural in the first place.

One of the joys of teaching is seeing the light come into a student's eyes and hearing that sigh of relief when I simply relax his wrist and elbow over to the left without changing the position of the viola. He then realizes that his arm, hand, and fingers are comfortable and that the natural finger contact on the string is with the fleshy part rather than with the extreme tip—a definite advantage for sound on the viola. This position is so natural and easy. Why should it come as a sudden revelation to so many? Because of the Golden(?) Rule: "Keep that elbow under." If these players could relax the left arm, let it drift to the left as they go across to the higher strings, they could play on each string with the same arching, the same point of contact, the same feeling on each string—and, most important, the same rich, mellow sound.

The left arm should be under the instrument as much as is required by the fingers, *and no more*. This means, of course, that it must be well underneath when playing on the C-string, especially in the upper positions, and even more so when reaching for an extension with the fourth finger. The left arm should relax as the fingers go to the higher strings, and then, of course, it must come under again as the fingers continue into the higher positions, where the hand needs to get around the body of the instrument. Here, it is not enough that the arm merely come under more, it must also come up so that the hand may rise over the body of the instrument—but that is another matter.

The important point to remember is that while water does seek its own level and the elbow does need to be under the fiddle (generally), the left arm must be flexible. It must be as relaxed as possible at all times and come under more only to meet the requirements of the fingers.

Another thing that is almost universally taught is to "leave the fingers down." I can see why this is necessary in the early stages. The beginner has no feeling for a set hand and arm position and if he lifted one finger when placing another, the hand and arm would probably center on the new finger. It would probably be impossible for the teacher to mold the pupil's hand into a proper first-position alignment. Another reason for the "leave the fingers down" admonition is that the pupil's ear is not yet developed. He is likely to be careless about exact pitch. The teacher feels that if he can get the pupil to leave the fingers down on the correct pitches on the way up the scale, then they will be in tune on the way down. This is fine and probably quite necessary—for beginners. As a matter of fact, any fine string player will do this when he is playing fairly rapidly and will have to play the same notes descending that he just played ascending, but this procedure is not necessary and is often detrimental when playing slowly and expressively with vibrato.

The best and most natural sound is produced with one finger at a time. The wrist vibrato, especially in the case of the fourth finger, is limited in scope when all the fingers are down. The most harmful manifestation of leaving unnecessary fingers down is tension, particularly in the case of those students who tend to press the fingers down hard—and I'm afraid that means most of them. Time after time, a new student will play a slow scale for me, leaving each finger glued to the string (and pressing that string into the fingerboard) until the fingers are needed for a note on the next higher string. Fortunately, this cannot be done on the way down because each finger has to be lifted in order for the next one to sound. One of my first teachers told me that leaving fingers down was an aid to facility and speed because the fingers were already there when you needed them to go down the scale. To this day, I cannot appreciate the advantage of being able to play down the scale faster than you can play on the way up!

One of my pet peeves that derives from the "leave the fingers down'' syndrome is the sloppy passagework and unwanted grace notes I hear so often from new students. In playing a rapid group of four sixteenths such as: c d e c (2 3 4 2), they provide me with a bonus—a fifth note in the group of four, a little grace note d between the e and c, a little mess between the third and fourth notes in the group. Since such composers as Haydn, Mozart, and Beethoven wrote thousands of such note-groupings, I get to hear this bonus quite often, in fact, *ad nauseam*. What amazes me is that I'm the only one who seems to notice. The student never seems to know what I'm talking about when first I bring this to his attention.

If you play 2 3 4 2 rapidly, leaving the third finger down while you play the fourth, and then try to lift 3 and 4 simultaneously, the sound probably isn't going to be clean. The fourth finger is shorter than the third and comes off more easily (it has a greater distance to go when lifted because of the alignment of the hand), thus the third-finger grace note.

I try to have my students lift the third finger while the fourth is down so as to avoid the mess between 4 and 2. The third finger does not have to be lifted high; in fact it can't be, it just has to be released. More often than I would care to say, the students are simply unable to lift the third finger while the fourth is down, so deeply ingrained is the habit of leaving the fingers down. They can lift the third if they also lift the second, but that should not be necessary, nor is it desirable. However, I would advise lifting both 2 and 3 when 4 is down if that is the only alternative to producing the unwanted grace note.

The same thing often happens with 1 2 3 1 groups and even with 0 1 2 0 groups. Here the cure is easier because no one has much trouble learning to lift 2 while 1 and 3 are down, and lifting 1 when only 2 is down is no problem at all. Nevertheless, I often have to point out the grace-note mess when these fingerings are used. Students have to practice lifting the fingers that tend to produce unwanted notes before those fingers can do damage.

Another undesirable manifestation of "leave the fingers down" occurs when playing chords. It seems the most natural thing to me to lift the finger or fingers on the lower two strings when the bow has already rolled over to the upper two. But student after student plays on the upper strings with the fingers still glued to the lower ones— with the arm too far under for the upper strings, the fingers on the upper strings tense and cramped, finger contact on the very tips, tight and narrow vibrato (if any at all)—and complains about how hard it is to play chords in tune!

When breaking four-string chords into two and two (which is the way they are almost always performed), it is not necessary to place the upper-string fingers until the bow is rolling over to those strings. Then those fingers can be placed with the left arm relaxed over to the left so that the point of contact is with the fleshy part of the fingers (the arm, hand, and fingers relaxed), and with the lower strings released so that a good, rich vibrato can be produced for the duration of the chord. Naturally, this applies to three-string chords as well. The basic rule is: Release the finger that you no longer need to depress, especially if it causes discomfort or technical difficulty.

Also, when playing arpeggiated chords, as in *Harold in Italy* by Berlioz, it is sometimes advantageous to lift fingers from the lower strings while the bow is on the upper strings and vice versa. This aids intonation, enables the hand and fingers (and arm) to remain relaxed, and often permits easy replacement on new notes when the chord changes in the middle of a group of sixteenths.

There is a passage in the first movement of the Bartók Viola Concerto (on the fifth page of the solo part) that consists of arpeggiated chords across the four strings, articulated as two notes slurred and two separate. These chords lie in the fourth, fifth, and sixth positions and are full of perfect fifths. Student after student has told me that this passage is impossible, and, indeed, it would seem so at first glance. I remember my first encounter with these chords. When I tried to play the fifths, the finger would go down between the two strings. Of course, the harder I pressed, the more the finger went between the strings, separating them even more.

The solution to the problem of the fifths lies in using minimal finger weight and lots of flesh contact with the strings and, most important, a flexibly rolling left arm. Actually, the flexible left-arm concept enables you to deal with one string at a time, literally rolling the finger from one string to another. The left arm, in general, should be "under more" for the lower strings, should relax to the left for the upper strings. When one has a freely rolling left arm and lifts the fingers not required at the moment (especially the fingers that are about to be used on other strings), the entire passage becomes eminently playable—clean and with correct intonation. Of course, it is the lifting of the fingers that *enables* the arm to roll freely. The technique does take practice and coordination. It is not easy, but neither is it "impossible."

I have already alluded to "pressing the strings into the fingerboard." I suppose that this is another of those necessary evils. The beginner has weak, undeveloped fingers that are likely to wander from the pitch if insufficient pressure is maintained on a given note, but I wish that students would not exaggerate the benefit of pressure to the extent that it becomes a problem for the rest of their lives.

I was specifically told by one of my early teachers that the softer I played, the harder I should press my fingers down. I understand why this was told to me. The excitement and intensity of playing loudly would insure sufficient pressure to keep the finger in place, whereas playing softly might cause me to let up on the weight too much. But the advice to press hard is very bad advice, indeed.

Pressing too hard builds calluses on the fingertips, digs grooves in the fingerboard, and wears the strings and causes them to become false. Much worse: it causes tension in the fingers and hand, which affects the vibrato and the shifting technique. I advise my students to experiment in order to determine how little finger weight they need to produce a clear sound. I have them play something fast, an etude or a perpetual motion, with no finger weight at all, to begin with. This produces whistles and harmonics, for they are just playing on the surface of the strings. Then I tell them to increase the weight of the fingers gradually. To their surprise, they find that almost immediately, before the strings have begun to touch the fingerboard, they have already achieved clarity in sound and pitch. I then advise them to go beyond that and depress the strings all the way, so that the strings make contact with the fingerboard. This insures that there will be enough downward pressure. Sometimes, when the vibrato is very fast and intense, I advise using a little extra weight to insure that the finger will remain anchored. But I certainly do not believe in pressing hard at any time, and I advise using less weight when playing fast passages where no vibrato is involved.

This is one area in which I'm a real nag as a teacher. It isn't easy to keep from pressing too hard with the fingers, and students need constant reminders to relax the finger weight, especially when shifting.

After all these years of knowing better, I still catch myself digging the string into the fingerboard in moments of great musical intensity. It is a continuing battle to remain physically relaxed when in the throes of intense emotional climax, but that is what produces the most effective result on the viola.

I teach tone production through relaxed weight of the bow arm. The arm rests on the bow through the index finger of the right hand; and the weight of the arm is directed onto the string by the arched right thumb, on the underside of the stick to the right of the index finger. This sounds complicated on paper, but it is very natural, and it is the way most fine violists play, whether or not they think about it in those terms. I believe that it is very healthy to think about it in exactly that way. The more sound desired, the more weight is *relaxed* onto the string—through the first finger. If the bow arm is more relaxed, it is likely that the left hand will be relaxed and that the fingers will not dig the string into the fingerboard.

On the viola it is very important to play with the flat hair in the upper half of the bow, with the wood directly above the hair. (I was taught by my first teacher to play with the stick turned away, to play on the "outside" of the hair. But I can't fault my teacher in this case, for I started on the violin.) Most people think that the big difference between the violin and the viola is felt in the left hand, for the notes seem to be so far apart on the viola. True, the reaches are greater for the left hand, and a violinist with small hands will have quite a problem trying to adjust to a viola. But a bigger problem would be having short arms, for the real difference in feel between the violin and the viola lies in the bow arm, in the distance between the body and the point where the bow and the string meet. When I try to play a violin, I feel as though I'm bowing right under my nose. The violinist trying a good-sized viola for the first time will find that he has to reach way out to place the bow between the bridge and the fingerboard. To make matters worse, the viola generally responds better when played farther away from the bridge than is the case with the violin. Therefore, while it is possible (perhaps preferable for people with longer arms) to play the violin with the bowstick turned away and still produce a big, relaxed sound, that is not advisable when playing the viola.

If one is to produce the sound by relaxing the weight of the bow arm downward, it is necessary to have the right wrist low in the upper part of the bow, especially at the tip. With the wrist down, the entire right arm feels its weight being relaxed downward; and with a relaxed right arm, a relaxed left arm is achieved naturally. Playing with the flat hair in the upper part of the bow is the way to attain this relaxed feeling.

Of course, when approaching the frog on an up-bow stroke, the stick may be (in fact, must be) turned away. But at the frog great weight is not needed, and it is possible to maintain a relaxed wrist and arm there even though the wrist may be quite high. Then, on the down-bow stroke, the stick should gradually be returned to the position in which it is exactly above the flat hair, at the same time the wrist gradually drops down in order to turn the stick. By the time the middle of the bow has been reached, the hair is again flat and the weight of the arm is again relaxed downward.

The turning of the bow toward the flat hair position and the lowering of the wrist on the down-bow stroke are not merely simultaneous. One is actually the cause of the other. The same thing is true on the up-bow stroke. On approaching the frog, the bow stick naturally turns away and the wrist naturally rises. I say that this happens ''naturally'' because it really does. Any attempt to fight this tendency by insisting that the hair remain flat all the way to the frog would result in a very uncomfortable sideways turn of the wrist.

One area in which I'm very likely to suggest ''refinements'' is in shifting. When many of my new students first play for me, they have no shifting technique at all. In fact, many of them have no legato either. They jump quickly from one position to another, making no connection between the notes involved and often releasing the weight on the bow as they jump from one note to another, thus insuring a complete disconnection. The modern student is so afraid that the shift might be heard, that he doesn't shift at all. The fear is founded, I believe, on the way that shifting is usually taught.

Perhaps it is necessary to teach an entirely ''positional'' method of shifting at first, in order to get the concept of positions across to the student. I was certainly taught that way. I remember being told that to go from an e (first finger, first position on the D-string) to a b (third finger, third position on that same D-string), it was necessary to slide my first finger up to a g, so that my hand would be in the third position, and then I could plop my third finger down on the b. In other words, in order to play an e going to a b on the same string, I had to play a little g in between.

That wasn't so bad. Of course, there was no g grace note between the e and the b in the music, but g *is* between e and b, and there might be an e minor chord involved, so what harm could the little g do? (Kreisler used to make shifts like that sound gorgeous.) But now consider this: A shift down from g (first finger, third position on the D-string) to an f♯ (second finger, first position on that very same D-string), a shift of a half-step! I was taught to slide my first finger (hand, arm, and all) down to an e in the first position (that's where I was going, wasn't I?) and then to add the second finger on the f♯! Now that is another matter. There is no e between g and f♯. In fact, there is no room for anything between g and f♯. Can you imagine what that kind of half-step shift sounded like? Is there any wonder that students spent the rest of their lives trying to obliterate the sound of such shifts?

I do not teach "positional" shifting. I have nothing against positional alignment of the hand. In fact, I insist on it. A positional concept is absolutely necessary for knowledge and mastery of the fingerboard, for fingering concepts, for control of intonation, and for stability and solidity of the left hand, in general. But one should not shift from one position to another position. Shifting should be done from one note to another. Positions are for *being* somewhere, not for *going* there. It is really so utterly simple: you have notes to play and fingers to play them with. You do this by ear with a relaxed hand and everything falls into place, naturally and easily.

Let's go back to the little half-step shift from g with the first finger back to f♯ with the second finger. Positionally (third position to first position), it is a shift of a minor third. But if you think just of the notes you have to play and the fingers involved, you only have to drag the first finger back (releasing the weight) a half-step to f♯ and replace it with the second finger. Of course, the first finger must move back (with no weight at all) a little farther in order to make room for the second finger on f♯, but not nearly as far back as e! Then, with the second finger already sitting on the f♯, relax the hand and arm back into the first position so that you can play an e with the first finger if you need to. But no extraneous pitch will have been heard between the g and the f♯, and there is no need to hide the sound of the shift or risk destroying the legato connection between the two notes.

I teach shifting in three steps: relaxing the hand in the direction of the shift before leaving the old note, relaxing the finger weight during the actual transfer of the new finger to the new note, and relaxing the hand and arm into the new position as soon as the new finger is in place so that one is ready to play the next note in the new position. After a while, steps two and three merge (the relaxing of the hand and arm taking place immediately, as soon as the new finger goes down on the new note). This leaves only the relaxing in the direction of the shift to be done in advance. There is some relaxed reaching toward the new note, which cuts down the actual distance traveled (without weight) by the old finger.

For example, in the shift from e to b (first finger to third on the D-string), the hand would be relaxed upward while the e was being played with the first finger. The third finger would be "aiming" (reaching in a relaxed manner) upward toward the b. The weight would then be released from the first finger as the hand and arm (led by the "aiming" third finger) pulled the first finger up to about an f♯ (the exact location does not matter). The weight and the concentration have already been shifted from the first finger to the third, which now goes down (with full weight) on the b. Then the hand and arm relax fully into the third position before another note is played.

The differences are that the hand does not go into the third position until after the b is reached with the third finger; the first finger does not travel as far before the third finger is placed; and the fleshy pad of the third finger goes down on the b because the finger was extended on the way up. The important advantage is that it is the *left* hand that releases and controls the weight during the shift, not the *right* hand. Most of my students have been taught (not by me!) to release the weight of the bow during the shift. This does the job all right. It hides the shift, but it also destroys the legato.

It isn't always such a great thing to hide the shift completely. Sometimes, in Romantic and modern music, a shift may be deliberately exposed to enhance the legato. When you have to change bow (because you're running out) and you don't want to change (because you want the line to go on) there is nothing like a rich, juicy shift to bridge the change of bow and continue the legato line.

Another thing that many of my students have been taught is to shift *quickly*. This goes along very well with the *jump* school, where there is no shift at all—just a quick skip to the new position. It is true, of course, that if you're going to disconnect, it is better to get it over with quickly and get on with the legato as soon as possible. But, unfortunately, the faster the shift the more likely it is to miss. Also, I find that a fast shift in a slow tempo is jarring and out of place. It can seriously upset a quiet, relaxed mood.

It is difficult for a student who has been taught to shift quickly to unlearn this habit. I ask my students to practice scales slowly in order to develop the habit of taking time for leisurely shifts from the note just before the shift. They return a week later with very slow scales but with shifts occurring at the last possible moment and as fast as ever. It takes a while for them to develop the ability to control the timing of the shift and to do it correctly with evenness, smoothness, grace, and accuracy. Once developed, however, this ability is a real asset. The student feels that he always has plenty of time for the shift, even when playing very rapid scales, and he does not feel pressured or hurried.

The shift should blend into the tempo and mood of the phrase. It should not be a technical maneuver but a part of the musical expression. In this way, it becomes unobtrusive in the *real* sense. It is there but it does not detract from the music or get in the way. It adds to the mood and shape of the music.

Another thing that I was taught and that I have "refined" is the vibrato. When I was a student (in the 1930s) there was a fairly universal prejudice against the use of arm vibrato, especially on the violin. I had developed a natural arm vibrato that produced a very lush tone. This, undoubtedly, was one of the factors that contributed to my ultimate preference for the viola, for my vibrato produced a sound that was very attractive on the viola, but it often sounded sluggish, too wide, and "too fat" on the violin.

Long before I had ever heard of the viola, my early violin teachers tried to "get rid of" my arm vibrato and insisted that I learn to vibrate from the wrist. It was a difficult period, but I worked very hard and finally developed a useful wrist vibrato. I have never been sorry about that, but I am very happy that I never got rid of my natural arm vibrato.

The prejudice against the arm vibrato has largely fallen by the wayside. Hundreds of fine young violinists today (not to mention violists) have good-sounding and efficient-looking arm vibratos and use no wrist at all. Strangely enough, I think that they are missing a good bet. The wrist vibrato and the arm vibrato each have their special advantages, so obviously the violist who has the two types is more fortunate, both expressively and physically, than his colleagues who have only one. The muscles used to generate the wrist vibrato are different from those that produce the arm vibrato. Therefore, while one set of muscles is at work, the other is at rest. The violist who has a choice can go on playing all day (and professional musicians often do) without becoming physically tired.

It might be well to clarify a matter of nomenclature at this point. The two types of vibrato are popularly known as the "wrist" vibrato and the "arm" vibrato. It would make just as much sense to call them the "hand" and the "shoulder" vibrato. It is the hand that vibrates from the wrist as a joint. The arm vibrates from the shoulder as a joint.

The obvious advantage of the wrist vibrato is that the hand is a much smaller piece of equipment than the arm. When great speed is desired in the vibrato (for great intensity), the hand is much more efficient than the arm, and much more comfortable. However, most people with exclusive wrist vibratos avoid using the fourth finger on expressive notes because the vibrato is too narrow and the fourth-finger sound is thin. Unfortunately, I know too many "three-fingered" violists with pure wrist vibratos.

With an arm vibrato, one can produce all the width one needs with any finger, including the fourth. One can also produce a rich sound when playing octaves or thirds or, in general, when two or more fingers are down at the same time. With the arm, one can continue to vibrate with a rich sound while making extensions, up or back.

By varying the speed and width of the vibrato, one can produce a myriad of colors and moods. It really does not matter whether the vibrato is being produced by the hand or by the arm; nor does it matter which finger is being employed. What matters is "how fast" and "how wide." The method of producing the vibrato may be changed from note to note or even on the same note. If the speed and width of the vibrato remain the same, it should be possible to change in mid-note from arm to wrist or from wrist to arm without a noticeable change in the sound.

When I play (even when I practice) I give no thought to whether I am using wrist or arm. I think only of the kind of sound I want—the kind of mood, color, and intensity, and whether the phrase is growing or relaxing. The method of producing the vibrato (wrist or arm) on any given note happens automatically and without any awareness on my part. If you were to ask me, after I had just played a phrase, which type of vibrato I had used on a given note, I would probably not have the slightest idea. I believe that this is as it should be. When one performs, one should be concerned with music, not mechanics.

Of course, to reach this stage, one must learn to vibrate with the wrist and with the arm, learn to control the speed and width in both cases, and practice to increase the speed and/or the width. I encourage most of my students to learn both types of vibrato. Usually they come to me with a definite inclination for one or the other, and, I must admit, they usually leave me with that same inclination. That's fine! What they are doing is natural for them and enables them to sound their best. Some exceptional students actually do develop both kinds of vibrato. Some actually come to me with both kinds (although some of them do not realize it). At any rate, I try to develop an arm vibrato to go with a natural wrist vibrato and a wrist vibrato to augment a natural arm vibrato. I do *not* discourage the natural vibrato and I do *not* try to get the student to *change* to the other type.

Most of the time this sort of thing happens: A student will come to me with an arm vibrato that is stiff and tight. I will explain and demonstrate both types of vibrato and give him material to practice and develop both types. I will encourage him to develop a wrist vibrato as well as to improve his arm vibrato. He may or may not develop a useful wrist vibrato, but, even if he doesn't, he usually winds up with a much freer, more relaxed, more versatile arm vibrato; and from working on the wrist vibrato, he will usually develop a relaxed wrist joint, which adds a dimension to the arm vibrato, if nothing more.

Similarly, the student with the wrist vibrato is encouraged to develop an arm vibrato, as well as to improve his wrist vibrato. He may gain an arm vibrato or he may feel much more comfortable with his natural wrist vibrato. What often happens is that he learns to use the arm with the fourth finger and/or in the upper positions, where the wrist is so bent that it can hardly be used.

Lots of good may be accomplished by encouraging both types of vibrato. In any case, no harm can be done as long as the student is encouraged to keep and improve his *natural* vibrato.

I would like to make this personal request to viola teachers: If you continue to teach a student beyond the beginning years, modify some of the things that you taught him initially. Explain to him why you taught him certain things at first and why you are now suggesting some refinements and exceptions. Tell him why you had to teach him that water seeks its own level, and show him why you now have to teach him about capillary attraction.

Janos Starker

An Organized Method of String Playing

Since 1955 I have been giving string seminars regularly on four continents under the title "An Organized Method of String Playing." The following is an attempt to describe what takes place in these public classes.

INTRODUCTION

"An Organized Method of String Playing" (OMSP) is a way of thinking about music and instrumental playing. Its objectives answer professional needs: stability, power, health, maximum use of limited time, increase of confidence and avoidance of stagnation, deterioration, nervousness, and insecurity. Though these needs are based on varying degrees of talent and ability, physical and/or musical, they are aggravated by previous learning processes. The necessary imitative learning of a child is too often continued into adulthood. Changes from concerned to unconcerned teachers, or vice versa, result mostly in the unexplained use of various schools of learning. These schools, often marvelously demonstrated by highly gifted exponents, reflect solutions of the exponents' individual shortcomings or advantages. In order to explain the thinking process behind the approach to OMSP, let me give some background as to its origin.

As a child prodigy from the age of six, I was fortunate in having a great teacher, Adolf Schiffer, a student and successor of David Popper. His forte was in assisting his students develop their natural abilities. He was a superb cellist and musician, but because of a rather late start as an instrumentalist, he limited his performing activities to string quartet playing. He used no method. He assigned

133

material, corrected musical errors, played fragments to clarify his suggestions, and ridiculed unnatural motions that were contrary to the music. Theatricality was discouraged and dismissed as fitting only for clowns to employ in lieu of talent. Inborn or inbred eccentricities when coupled with talent were considered sufficient to reach recognized stage heights.

Two other exceptional teachers to whose wisdoms I had access were Leo Weiner (piano chamber music) and Imre Waldbauer (string quartets). Weiner, a composer and a mediocre but functional pianist with a powerful musical mind and incredibly disciplined ears, taught his disciples to hear. Waldbauer, a highly respected violinist of his renowned string quartet, had a scientific mind and was preoccupied with the various mechanical ways of producing sounds. He clarified the need for and the possibility of verbal definitions based on experience and on the works of Hugo Riemann and Friedrich Adolph Steinhausen.

After I had reached instrumental maturity and control of a large part of the repertory, World War II caused a year of absence from my instrument. Following this silence I had but two weeks to prepare for my first public appearance. I continued the profession successfully, and shortly thereafter I occupied the solo cellist's post of the Opera and Philharmonic Orchestra of Budapest. A year or so later I found myself listening to a recital in Vienna. One of the most admired instrumentalists of our time was performing, a legendary former child prodigy. His left hand was vibrating indiscriminately and barely managed to arrive at the necessary destinations. A loud irregular breathing penetrated the entire hall. I left in the intermission on the verge of nausea. We are all aware of the pressures of international concertizing and reluctantly accept the fact of human frailty, justifying an occasional "off night." A series of sleepless nights forced on me the realization that the occurrences at that concert involved issues far beyond an "off night." I had nightmarish visions of the legendary peasant eye surgeon who, when told of the dangers involved in his activities, was never able to repeat his feats. The historically low percentage of child prodigies who grow up to be mature artists needed explanation, and it became imperative to have an acceptable reasoning as to what governs the satisfactory mental and physical functions of a performing artist when called on stage.

Through some horror-laden months of ineffective public experimentation, followed by a long stretch of self-imposed inactivity, I became aware that only through conscious understanding of the elements that allow music to be produced on an instrument can one become a professional and reasonably independent of the constant hazards. Only through conscious understanding can one control the "skill" part of producing art and distinguish the gifted dilettante from the master professional. This realization induced me to search for the "basic" problems involved in playing an instrument; basic problems that are identical for all and inherent in all music irrespective of subjective feelings and judgments. Invariably, when that search reached the point where the problem was defined, solutions presented themselves, explaining and justifying the differing approaches. Invariably, advantages and disadvantages appeared that were humbling to those whose religious fervor for a chosen route deterred all contradictions, while for those with vastly different abilities answers were provided.

The emphases on professionalism are manifold. Regardless of whether a musician performs as a soloist or as a member of a small or a large ensemble, or assists a budding instrumentalist in learning the "trade," the significance of understanding and knowledge of the issues involved is far beyond the value of natural gifts. It would be infantile to discount the lack of democracy in the distribution of talents; however, the goal toward maximum utilization of one's gifts is universal. When talent and fortunate circumstances coincide, there may be no need for theories in order to arrive at great results. Those who are satisfied with their output would never bother about problems, since they do not have them. On the other hand, only those are safe from fear who do not realize the risks involved; risks, not necessarily personal, but artistic. It is one thing to lose a competition or audition because of an inferior showing, and another not to win over someone equally good or better. The risks are that of self-respect, and above all the respect for music itself. One ought to be nervous before a performance to some degree, not because of fear of the unknown but because of one's respect for the significance of artistic contribution.

ORGANIZATION

After years of investigation I was able to place the various problems in some obvious categories. This categorizing alleviated the
universal plague of lack of practice time. I would venture to say that
there is no musician who has not said on occasion, "If I'd had more
time I could have. . . ." We may deplore the lack of time for all
human endeavors that aim toward unreachable goals, but the misuse
of time is just as tragic. It is quite usual for a player who practices
one hour to spend half that period repeating already well controlled
passages and melody lines. Commonplace is the player who
endlessly repeats a difficult passage without realizing that the problem is not a left-hand one, but lies in the bowing, string-changing,
phrasing, grouping, or holding of the instrument, and so ad
infinitum.

The four categories are: I. Playing Preparation, II. Right Arm–
Hand–Fingers, III. Left Arm–Hand–Fingers, IV. Musical Application. The order and titles are clearly arbitrary. The fourth group,
musical application, could obviously be first, or should it be? It
ought to be taken for granted that all aspects of instrumental playing
must be motivated by musical intentions. To play in tune, to produce
uninterrupted lines, to eliminate scratchy sounds, to guard against
uncontrolled dynamic changes due to changes in bow speed, and to
avoid unwritten notes while connecting distant intervals are not
technical demands but musical ones. The solutions are technical,
nevertheless. So in order to fulfill the inner musical needs, physical
conditions must be as close as possible to the ideal so as to allow the
musical ideal to emerge.

A passage that contains even units should be played evenly. The
execution requires technical answers; the motivation remains musical. The element of freedom, the beauty of individual interpretation
of black and white notes is taken for granted. However, freedom of
interpretation does not justify anarchy due to technical shortcomings. *Rubato* is freedom within the phrase: *agogic* is freedom
within the bar. The meaning is clear. Notes lengthened or shortened
because of melodic, harmonic, rhythmic, and emotional significance
must be balanced so as to preserve the structural unity of phrases

and movements. Myriads of individual varieties are within the realm of possibility without destroying the essential balance. Such an approach requires discipline, primarily oral, but in order for the oral senses to function, one needs physical and mental discipline. Well known is the player who hears what he imagines in his inner ear instead of what emanates from his instrument. Well known is the player who thinks that everybody else is too slow, while he races indiscriminately through his passages. Well known is the stage in learning a work when one can only play the difficult passages fast, as the digital learning precedes the musical learning. In other words, discipline must be the basis of one of the classic disciplines, music, and once attained, freedom of expression may spring forth.

The order of learning is significant. Beautiful artistic ideas running rampant without disciplined instrumental control remind one of a ride in a magnificent automobile over unpaved roads. Writing poetry in a language yet unlearned seldom succeeds. One must be acquainted with vowels and consonants, so as to form syllables, words, and sentences. Then poetry may eventually emerge. The cold-bloodedness vaguely implied in this approach is a matter to be considered, but only in the light of professionalism versus dilettantism, and some further reference will be made to this when the fourth group is discussed.

Artistic motivation should be understood as the drive toward purity, simplicity, and structure in re-creating masterpieces. Underlying these motivations is what one may call the basic or ideal legato: undisturbed musical sounds that linearly ascend or descend; harmonic successions that continue toward focal points, climactic or anticlimactic; rhythmic consistencies—pulses that are not interfered with by changing rhythms; dynamic contrasts based on musical content and not on impressive volume effects; and, finally, recognition of the inherent voice examples that are the basis of all musical aspirations.

With these thoughts in mind it may be evident that the attempt to describe OMSP is doomed to partial success at best. Instrumental playing is based on multiple sensations. One may hint at them and induce them on occasion, but ultimately each individual must arrive at these sensations on his own. That is why the maximum results obtained by this thinking process are accomplished in seminars where the participating groups experiment, observe, and, on occasion, discover that some of these "sensations" are either novelties or elements that are known but ignored. None of the problems discussed are original in either their statement or their solution. They are based on previously known principles. The order in which they are proposed is intended to show the interrelations leading to desired musical results.

Category I: Playing Preparation

The problems in the first category involve the use of the muscles and the application of power and weight, as well as motions, balance, breathing, and timing; the last with special consideration of conscious anticipation and delay of all actions.

I have always been preoccupied with the idea that the energy spent to supply the physical needs of playing an instrument should be minimal and thereby allow the mental and emotional faculties to function freely for the sake of communicating the musical message. The visible struggle of a performer may create sympathy, but it has little if anything to do with music. In the field of stagecraft this sympathy can serve us well when the musical message lacks conviction. The adrenaline expended by a perspiring, contorting performer often substitutes for artistic substance. In order to use only the minimum energy required, one must have maximum power available at all times and use only what is necessary.

The power is aimed at the contact points on the strings, via the bow and the left fingers. The power of the arm originates in the back muscles. The goal, therefore, is not to hinder the flow of energy from the source. It seems obvious that if the fingers, hands, forearms, upper arms, and shoulders function without the support of the back muscles, the locally used energy will have to increase proportionately.

"Relaxed" playing is in reality the even distribution of muscle tension. Though we are playing an instrument while "making" music, the playing requires power and precludes relaxation. To attain this even distribution of muscle tension we should try to locate the hindrances. Wherever joints meet there is a tendency to disrupt the flow of tension by unequal tensing of the next set of muscles, and forming what we may call angles. The most frequent trouble spots are the shoulder, the forearm (when opening), the thumb, and the muscles beneath the knuckles. We should attempt to avoid angular formations and to create the feeling of curves. At the same time, whenever possible, descending lines should be formed by both arms, as a further means of avoiding the disruption of continuous energy flow. Of course it is impossible for the left arm to create descending lines when playing the violin, the viola, or the first few positions on the cello.

Two simple exercises will help one to recognize the different sensations of this angular versus curved feeling. (1) Raise both shoulders very high, pull the arms back, rotate the arms inward, bring them forward at skull level while bringing the backs of the hands together, then drop both arms to their respective instrumental playing positions, so as to promote the active participation of the back muscles. (2) Tense the upper arm muscles as much as possible but avoid any tension in the hand and fingers. This maximum tension should result in a shaking forearm. Then make a fist. Gradually squeeze the fingers in the fist and slowly open the forearm to allow the upper arm tension to travel into the fist. The natural tendency to tighten the upper arm excessively to produce stronger dynamics and also the crucially wrong tendency of automatically tightening the forearm muscles when accelerating should, by this exercise, be reduced and make one aware of these misuses of tension.

The application of weight can be approached through the suspension of the arms. Again, when lifting the arms, the back muscles, not those of the upper arm, are required for the necessary power. Prior to lifting, total relaxation is experimented with, with the limbs and body devoid of any tension, and only the legs holding the body while standing. The difference in the sensations of weight and pressure in preparation for the eventual needed mixture is advanced in this way.

The ability to apply power to the changing needs of playing high strings, low strings, high positions, and low positions requires the ability to shift the body weight without losing control, ipso facto, balance. The following simple exercise will aid in achieving controlled body balance: Stand, place the weight of the body on the right side, lift the left leg, bend the right knee. Repeat a few times until reasonably comfortable. Repeat the same exercise on the left side using the right leg. Then, while seated on the edge of a chair, place the right foot in the center, lift the left leg, and rise on the right foot. Repeat with the left foot. The difficulties encountered will make one aware of the lack of body control, ill-directed body weight, and the need to feel the changing balance requirements.

Breathing, that is, the use of controlled breathing, can be approached by various means. The general tendency to use excessive speed at the start of all actions is demonstrated by the quick intake of air when inhaling and, similarly, when exhaling. The following exercises divide the amount of air into even groups of 4, 6, 8, 12, 16, 24, etc. Starting with empty lungs, sip air audibly and check the speed of the air intake, with the predetermined group in mind, so as to finish with the lungs completely filled. Do the same while exhaling. Later, when experimenting with control of bow speed, practice synchronizing the division and speed of the bow with exhaling and inhaling.

Lack of controlled breathing results in other noticeable disturbances: Holding the breath while playing difficult passages causes incorrect accents, unplanned groupings of passages, and, most important of all, unprepared starts of phrases and changes. Anticipation of all actions is of the utmost significance in all phases of instrumental playing and music making. The word *anticipation* is used in the sense of preparation, in contrast to delay. The following sentence seems to define the need: Anticipation is part of music itself; therefore it must bear all the characteristics of the music that follows—time, dynamics, melody, and harmony. The start of a phrase requires an anticipatory, preparatory upbeat or cue. This cue must reflect the basic unit of the phrase. A change of character requires a preparatory cue with the change inherent in it. A bow change requires the preparation of directional change. String changes require preparation of the new bow level. Position changes require preparation of the new arm position. Speed changes require preparation of the necessary tension adjustments. If the breathing is not hindered these anticipations can be consciously assisted by the proper intake of air. Naturally, through some training, most of these actions become subconscious, and only in extreme difficulties and in the practicing process, does one need the conscious application.

Anticipation is clearly responsible for uninterrupted, continuous, fluent actions, and in a musical sense I like to refer to its result as legato, in contrast to the marcato character resulting from delayed actions.

By now it should be evident that the language employed to describe OMSP deliberately avoids the use of scientific terms. It is the language applied in the classroom during seminars, where the visual and audible aspects are stressed in the form of examples of right and wrong, pleasant and unpleasant, convincing and unconvincing, struggling and effortless, and so on.

In group discussions many of the issues intertwine, as in actual application. For instance, how one holds the instrument belongs to the first category, playing preparation. Nevertheless, it is usually discussed either when the basic legato is explored, or when the guiding principles of the use of the left hand are negotiated. The reason for this is (1) to accommodate the changing requirements of the bow on different strings, and (2) to provide a basis for the left hand so that the fingers can stop the string at an identical angle in all positions.

In the seminars the following elements are experimented with in an effort to find suitable positions for the differing needs of each individual: One must first, as in the balance experiment, secure the ability, seated or standing, to shift the weight of the body left or right at will; second, secure the unhindered function of the arms; and third, confront the issue for cellists of the length of the end pin. This last item evokes intense debates in most seminars. The oversimplified answer as to whether to use the straight, the bent (Tortelier), or the excessively long end pin is that the height and the arm length of the player should be the deciding factors. Holding the instrument more vertically allows the average-sized person to concentrate the power on the contact point on the instrument. It has the disadvantage that the bow tends to slip downward; on the other hand, it makes easier all light, fast bowings and the synchronization of the so-called virtuoso elements. Holding the instrument more horizontally is an advantage for tall players with long arms, as they can use the forearm more comfortably because of the increased distance. The discomfort of holding the arms higher is compensated for by the ready effect of gravity, generally resulting in louder sound production. The ability to *see* the strings is of no consequence, unless it is a psychological advantage.

Therefore, the summation is that whichever end pin is used, it should not hinder the free motion of the arms. All positions should be within reach without the need to alter the body position. The instrument should not interfere with free breathing. The cello should be positioned in such a way that the knees can move it left and right without the upper half of the body moving. The knees should not cover the ribs of the instrument, thus muting the sound. At the same time the knees should be able to apply counterpressure, resistance against the bow, at will.

It is advisable to experiment with various heights of the chair (if it is not adjustable, a pillow or book can serve), until conscious body control is attained. It is of value to experiment with various leg placements and the proper part of the chair to occupy. With a standard end pin the experiments favor the front of the chair. The legs can be positioned either left foot forward on the heel, right foot quite far back on the toes, or the reverse. Both feet planted solidly better serve the users of the curved or long end pins.

Category II: Right Arm–Hand–Fingers

The second and fourth fingers of the right hand obtain the basic balance; the others transmit power. With the arm suspended, rest the bow flat on the second finger with the little finger counterbalancing on the top of the bow. After a somewhat secure feeling has been obtained, place the first and third fingers, then the thumb, and then grip solidly. Now switch the little finger to the outside into its regular position, without allowing the bow to tilt. A whipping hand motion will test whether the hold is secure enough to prevent the bow from slipping. The power of the arm is transmitted through the thumb and third finger for the down-bow, and through the thumb and first finger for the up-bow. Starting from the middle of the bow, the rotation of the forearm prepares for the next bow direction. Down-bow: pull the entire arm, gradually lift the upper arm, approximately at the middle start opening the forearm and continue to raise the upper arm until the tip of the bow is reached. Through the forearm rotation we arrive at the required position for the up-bow. Up-bow: start with a pushing action, close the forearm in, gradually lower the upper arm, and from approximately the middle of the bow, return the entire arm to

its original position. We say "approximately" because of the variations required by the different strings. This entire arm–forearm action defines the basic legato stroke.

The circular function of the arm, as with all limbs, would result in
a circular motion on the strings, unless the forearm takes over the
horizontal line. At the frog the weight of the arm through the bow,
combined with the speed of the motion, provides the required fric-
tion to set the string in vibration and establish sound. As the arm
increases its distance from the string, pressure substitutes for the
diminishing weight. The pressure travels through the third finger and
thumb, and, as the described arm function continues, in the up-bow
the first finger takes over the role of the third finger. The muscles
leading to the third finger and thumb are responsible for the power
while pulling. The muscles leading to the first finger and thumb are
responsible for the power while pushing (supination–pronation).
The bow should be at a 90° angle on the second string. On the cello
the angle of the bow should increase for the lower strings and de-
crease for the A-string. On the violin and viola the reverse is true.
This basic legato stroke, with the forearm opening and closing without a noticeable change in speed, should provide us with the basis
for almost all existing strokes.

I feel the need to remind the reader that this description of the
legato action is full of omissions and contradictions. However, the
purpose of this summary is not to disprove or replace any of the far
more scientifically correct writings on the subject. It is rather to
acquaint one with how, in seminars, problems are solved through
experiments, and how hoped-for results are obtained.

As the basic legato stroke is practiced slowly, attention should be
focused on the position of the arm at all points between the frog and
the point. Whatever stroke we use, and whatever part of the bow we
use, the arm should be in the position as established in the basic
legato stroke. If we play a series of staccato notes up-bow, when we
arrive at the middle the entire arm should gradually return to its
original position, while continuing the staccato to the frog. If we
start a note in the second half of the bow, the forearm should be in
"opened" position, and the upper arm accordingly at a higher level.
Higher than what? Higher than while playing in the first half of the
bow. All strokes that require the bow to leave the string must still

follow the same rule. While the bow is in the air the arm motion remains the same as if it were on the string. No change in speed should occur in the air unless the musical notation requires one, and, as such, demands preparation.

Bow changes, as well, must take place in the air if the preceding note has part of its value off the string. The spiccato stroke should be looked upon as a series of fast bow changes. In all bow changes the pressure of the thumb should be reduced immediately prior to the change. In the standard legato stroke the pressure applied through the thumb creates the unity of the forearm and the hand. Any sustained sound requires this unity, and in this sense I prefer to refer to it as sostenuto bowing. When the thumb pressure is reduced, and the forearm tension is reduced accordingly, the hand starts moving independently. As the forearm leads the repeated short notes up and down, with the hands in circular motion (almost no tension in the thumb), it will allow the bow to leave the string and thus spiccato will result. The experimentation is as follows: First, suspend the arm with no tension in any part of the arm or hand. Second, move the forearm horizontally left and right, and let the hand move as a consequence, hanging freely. Third, move the forearm up and down and allow the hand to move accordingly. Fourth, move the forearm clockwise and counterclockwise, allowing the hand to make similar circles. Always remember that it is not the hand that initiates the movements but the arm. Fifth, press the thumb to the index finger very strongly and try the horizontal movement again. As the hand does not move now, continue the arm movement, and gradually reduce the thumb pressure to the point where the hand starts moving again independently. Finally, with bow in hand on the string, try step five, starting at the balance point of the bow.

The placement of the thumb is approached with the idea that it should not be placed. When the hand hangs the thumb is in line with the first finger. When the forearm turns inward the thumb is in line with the second finger. The significant factor is that when the thumb is "pulled" toward the palm to be in line with the second finger immediate muscle tension results, and that should be avoided. The same is true for the left thumb placement.

In order to preserve the uninterrupted descending line of the arm it is necessary to clarify the role of the elbow and the wrist. Since both are joints, it is preferable to say "raise or lower the upper arm" instead of "raise or lower the elbow." Similarly, "raise or lower the hand," instead of "raise or lower the wrist." The multitude of bowings are discussed in terms of hard and soft consonant attacks, the length of the vowel content on the string, time spent on the string or in the air, stops with consonants or vowels, and notes ending with final consonants as in vocal use—*m* or *n*—so as to avoid dead sound stops.

The self-imposed limitations in the seminars prevent a detailed explanation and clinical description of the known bowings. The emphasis is on recognition, samples, and modes of experimentation. The most common problem, which is quickly recognized, is the lack of sufficient contact with the string toward the tip of the bow. One approach to curing this ailment is to have another person hold the tip of the bow while the player attempts to play an up-bow and a down-bow. If the hold is firm the player must exert considerably more power than usual. Then, in the form of isometric exercises, the player is asked to do the same, imagining that someone is holding the tip of the bow. When the contact is not sufficient, excess bow speed will create whistles instead of sounds; conversely, when too much pressure is applied without commensurate speed scratching will result.

Category III: Left Arm–Hand–Fingers

When the discussions of the OMSP reach this group a great number of issues are supposed to become self-explanatory. The principles governing the use of the arm, the shoulder, and forearm opening have been discussed in the first and second groups: to distribute muscle tension evenly, to keep from breaking the muscle line, to open the forearm continuously, to avoid all abrupt motions due to sudden changes in speed, to recognize the primary importance of avoiding angular tensing of the thumb in all positions, and to reduce forearm tension when playing fast passages. After all these questions have been defined and recognized, the placement of the fingers and the three different positions on the cello (versus practically only one on the violin and the viola) have to be explored.

Basically there are three different approaches in placing the fingers on a string: slanted backward; slanted forward, thus having a small finger contact point; and perpendicular, with maximum surface flesh contact. Each of these approaches has advantages and disadvantages, and affects the use and choice of vibrato, the various connections, slides, and the ability to explore all types of musical and virtuoso elements. The obvious suggestion is to master all three ways and apply them according to need.

The perpendicular hold serves well on thicker strings and in the first seven positions (positions counted by half-steps). The large surface contact on the strings gives a feeling of security, and the arm weight is used to more advantage, but when proceeding to higher positions, breaks in the motion and alterations in the sound quality occur. The intonation is considerably less exact than when the contact point is small, but that becomes an issue only on a very high level of music making, where clear overtone responses are aimed for.

The backward slant answers the shortcomings of the perpendicular hold; continuity all through the fingerboard is facilitated, and intonation is far more exact. The backward slant favors the use of the first and second fingers and their extensions. The forward slant favors the use of the third and fourth fingers and their extensions. The disadvantages occur in the lower positions, where the weight and pressure concentrate on a minute part of the fingertip and thus extreme exactness is required. With the perpendicular hold one is more likely to use hand vibrato, moving above and below the center and using the thumb, pressing on the neck, as an axis around which the hand rotates forward and backward. The slanted hold is more suited to arm vibrato, with the thumb only slightly touching the neck and moving with the hand and forearm in an identical direction. The hand–forearm unit is similar to that of the sostenuto sensation of the right arm.

Because of the greater tension used with arm vibrato, the application of indiscriminate vibrato to cover up intonation discrepancies is less likely. The vibrato, an element of decoration, should be applied to enhance the emotional content and to help the notes that are not enriched by natural overtones. Notes such as F, B, A flat, and E flat do not have corresponding overtones on a four-stringed instrument, while the notes that parallel the open strings and their harmonics have responding overtones. The vibrato should also be used to correct this tonal discrepancy. I rarely go beyond the rudimentary description of the various elements required in the use of vibrato. In group discussions and experimentations an attempt is made to discover what prevents the individual from functioning at will with a continuous motion. Once the problem is pinpointed, ways to improve are suggested.

In up-and-down glissandi, stop with finger pressure and try to continue the arm motion, as in back-and-forth glissandi. Place a finger on the back of the stretched-out right hand and try to obtain a feeling of continuous motion without the string-stopping pressure. Exchange fingers on the same note and try to maintain a uniform quality in the successive sounds through continuous motion.

Researchers, using complex machinery, have not yet come up with an agreed-upon analysis of the acoustical properties of vibrato. Therefore, we have to rely on our own audio mechanism, which is developed through individual experiences. At whatever stage that development takes us, we should try to satisfy the inner need, and then strive to expand it. This principle involves all aspects of playing music, and when our concern is the left hand, the inquiry turns to the geography of the fingerboard.

It is generally recognized that the basic, unalterable problem of intonation on a stringed instrument is the diminishing size of the intervals as the pitch rises. Since the frets of yesteryear are preserved only on the guitar, we should aim at developing a mental and physical keyboard on the fingerboard.

The first step is to accept the classification of standard and extended positions. The extended positions require unnatural hand positioning and are therefore dealt with as a deviation from the norm. In my belief they should be used only when they are unavoidable for technical or expressive reasons. On the first half of the cello, when the thumb is not used as a playing finger, we distinguish four-finger positions and three-finger positions. The placement of the first finger defines the position, and therefore it is preferable to name the positions according to the note played by the first finger, instead of the numbering based on the diatonic scale. This helps in visualizing the fingerboard as well as in memorizing. If the chromatic scale is used then we have eight four-finger positions, where the fingers are

each placed a half-step apart and enclose a minor third. From the
ninth half-step on, the fourth finger is seldom used, though it can be.
This area causes immense problems for cellists because of the transition of the thumb into thumb positions. Instead of leaving the
thumb in a sort of limbo, if we develop four distinct three-finger
positions, the thumb will adjust to a different placement on the side
of the neck, as in fluent preparation for the thumb position. The
development of the three-finger position (there are four of them,
because if the highest note played is a minor third above the octave,
there is no real need for a standard-sized hand to use the thumb on
the string) should immediately include the extensions for practical-
ity. The second finger is now a whole-step away from the first finger
rather than a half-step, and the enclosed interval remains a minor
third, as in the four-finger positions.

The thumb positions are identical with the standard positions on
the violin. The interval enclosed between the thumb and third finger
is a fourth. The name of the position is defined by the note played by
the thumb, and the distance between the first and second fingers can
change from a half-step to a whole-step. Thus many permutations
are possible, and a number of exercises have been devised, based on
this system. The exercises, no different from many in traditional
exercise books except in their mathematical formulae, are contained
in my book, *An Organized Method of String Playing—Cello Left
Hand Exercises.*[1] The book contains sample exercises to develop
the basic four-finger, three-finger, and thumb positions. For various
reasons double-stops are used for this development. First, the
greater number of fingers that sense a position the greater the security. Second, when playing double-stops, which constitute the major
part of a triad, one is more likely to be disturbed by discrepancies in
intonation that call for correction. Third, the sense of a note that
belongs to changing harmonies readies the player to observe this
essential element. When positions are approached with double-
stops, the enclosed intervals are considered on two strings. Therefore, in the four- and three-finger positions we speak of a seventh or
a major third, and in the thumb positions, octaves or seconds (4–1,
1–4, 3–1, 1–3, Q–3, 3–Q).

1. New York: Peer International, 1965.

Unfortunately the book omits double-stop exercises with open strings. These should be added by each individual. It is not absolutely necessary to practice all the permutative possibilities in a given position once they are recognized. Each player ought to develop a personal formula. To release the excess tension of double-stopping, single-note patterns are used to check the attained results. These single-note patterns are also more usable for less-advanced players with less-developed hands.

The second major step in developing a sense of geography on the fingerboard is the connecting of positions. Because the number of permutations runs into the millions—each note in each position, on each string, connecting to every other one—it will remain the promised land to attain total security forever. Frustrating? Yes, but providing a lifelong chance to progress, as long as the physical conditions are supportive.

The following elements should be observed while connecting positions: Reduce finger tension while traveling on a string. Concentrate on forearm opening and closing to sense the distance. Regardless of which finger goes to which finger, the distance should be based on the first finger's old and new positions, in other words, always connect positions instead of fingers or notes. Preserve the angle of the hand and fingers to the string. Rotate the forearm outward or inward according to the direction and according to the basic approach in finger contact. Anticipate all new positions by preparing the next position of the arm. The same goes for string changes.

Position changes require time just as all travel consumes time. Thus we distinguish two types of position connections, or slides, or shifts—anticipated and delayed. The anticipated "slide" takes its time from the first note. The finger that plays the first note slides. The next finger to play drops in place only on arrival, on the beat. If a bow change occurs between the two notes, the slide takes place on the first bow and the bow changes precisely on arrival with the next finger. The last element is the most frequently neglected. The so-called pure anticipated slides are those of lower fingers connecting to higher ones, and the same fingers connecting. Extreme care should be exercised when the same fingers are connecting, to reduce pressure on the string while traveling. Irrespective of the distances, close or far, these principles are essential. The opposite is true in the case

of delayed slides. The time is taken from the second note. The finger
to play the next note slides. The slide starts on the next beat. If a
bow change is needed, as in most cases, the slide is contained in the
next bow.

Combination slides are required when higher fingers change to
lower fingers (3 to 1, 4 to 3, 3 to 2, etc.) as anticipated slides. The
higher finger still leads the slide, but as close to arrival as possible
the next finger pushes out the previous one. On very distant connections the start may be anticipated and the arrival delayed. The decision of which type of slide to use should be based on musical taste.
The same goes for how much of the slide should be audible, or even
featured. The highly Italianate, crescendoed, backward slides are
disturbing to many of us, and seem to be a throw-back to the
nineteenth century. Russian musicians are fond of featured crescendoed slides, though most of Western literature seems to negate their
use. Reduced pressure of the bow while traveling will cover the
slide. Constant or increased pressure will display or feature the
slide. A variety of expressions can be attained simply by reapplying
pressure before arrival at different points.

To further left-hand security, the hand placement should aim the
fingers over two strings, or rather toward the fingerboard under two
strings. The feeling of walking a tightrope, when all the fingers hover
over one string, is thereby reduced. (This is one more reason for
practicing double-stops.) This two-string feeling in thumb positions
brings up a problem that is approached differently by the various
schools. The usual fifth hold of the thumb on two strings, providing a
constant position basis while the other fingers manipulate on the
neighboring string, tends to obliterate overtones on the lower string.
The thumb hanging in the air, or worse, tensing in the air, vastly
reduces security and induces greatly differing vibrato with the
changing fingers, but allows for richer overtone response and louder
sounds.

For a decade or so a quiet revolution has been in the making to
treat this issue, notwithstanding the traditional approaches in playing high positions. It proposes placing the thumb under the fingerboard and moving it there while playing the second half of the
fingerboard, thereby continuing the four-finger positions, and, as if
playing the violin, gradually including the distance of a fourth

between the first and fourth fingers. This approach seems to answer the question of security, the matter of the functioning overtones, and the need for an identical angle between the fingers and the strings in all positions. The disadvantages are caused by the characteristics of the traditional equipment of the cello—the thinness of the fingerboard and the sharp angularity of the block, which hinder the transition of the thumb from under the neck to under the fingerboard. It is my belief that changes will occur to rectify these obstacles and open up new vistas for technical progress on the cello.

Other elements concerning finger actions are: The intensity required to press down the strings should be directed into two fingers, the thumb and the playing finger. This creates a feeling of unity between the two. (A reminder—thumb tension should not be directed toward the neck.) The feeling of unity must constantly change to the finger that takes over. The takeover requires a release of tension in the previous finger and the immediate anticipated increase of tension in the next one. Dramatic harm is caused by retaining tension in one finger while another is called on to serve. The transfer of tension from one finger to another differs only in timing in the various applications. In sostenuto playing the release is delayed, and the next finger anticipates the tension. Therefore, for a short stretch, the two actions frequently intertwine. In the case of the vertical left-hand attack, for stronger impulses and especially for fast passage playing, the release is quicker, allowing the next finger to rise higher. From this height, weight and gravity will provide the needed power to stop the string.

The so-called percussion left-hand pizzicato is discussed in terms of its use when absolutely needed. Connections between fingered notes and open strings require it, primarily to assist the open string to speak. To strengthen the fingers, practice plucking leftward with the fingers. On occasion, a descending run can be clarified by applying this action, but one should not lose sight of the fact that the necessary excess tension will, in the long run, hinder the continuity of motion. The following exercise will focus on the changing tension requirements in the forearm when playing fast runs intermittently with held vibrated notes: a note is vibrated with the first finger, exaggerated tension is applied, then tension is released completely, a fast run of fingers 2–3–4–3–2–1 follows, and renewed vibrato and tension close. The next run is 1–2–3–4–3–2–1, without tension, closing with a vibrated and held second finger. The next finishes on the third finger, and so on; eventually we reach several repeated runs without tension before holding a vibrated note.

Another exercise to avoid cramping of the left hand when playing forte or stronger, is practicing fortissimo harmonics. It is just as necessary to avoid the frequent lack of sufficient finger pressure when playing piano, and this should be cured by playing forte in the left hand while using flautato with the bow.

At this stage in the discussion of OMSP, the seminar's attention is turned to such topics as harmonics, extensions, and pizzicato, although it seems logical that they be included in the second group, the right hand. In regard to harmonics, suggestions resort to elements already discussed. The primary reference is to the thumb position, where the enclosed interval of a fourth provides the intonation basis of harmonics, and the rest concerns the tension relationship of the thumb and the unpressed third finger. The significance of the bow speed, contact, and an undisturbed straight line are stressed and experimented with. The undisturbed straight line is required in all phases of string playing, but it is while playing harmonics that the player is likely to realize its significance and what tonal harm the lack of it can cause.

In regard to extensions, with repeated advice to avoid them whenever possible, the suggestion is made to rotate the hand so that the thumb gets closer to the third finger. This results in the feeling that the first finger is stretching back instead of the other fingers stretching forward. The moment when the stretch is not needed the first finger should move a half-step higher to obtain the feeling of the next position.

The two types of pizzicato—horizontal and melodic, or vertical and percussive—are then discussed, starting the experimentation with the hold of the bow. When fast arco–pizzicato exchange is called for the basic bow hold should not change radically. The first finger stretches out and the hand turns downward, allowing the first finger to touch the strings when needed and return for arco. For continuous pizzicato, the bow should be turned so the bottom part of the frog (called the slide) is pressed against the palm. The third and fourth fingers hold the bow, allowing the thumb to lean against the side of the fingerboard, while the first or second finger draws across the string or strings as if bowing toward the end of the fingerboard. This type of pizzicato, resulting in a melodic, ringing sound, is called for in most cases in the literature. Rhythmic percussive sounds are plucked vertically or semivertically. In fast pizzicato the thumb may support the plucking finger. Arpeggiated pizzicato uses the thumb upward and any of the fingers downward. Again this is a rudimentary approach to a complex area in which the demands of the literature bring recognition, experimentation, and decisions based mostly on individual taste.

It should be evident that aside from an occasional reference to the other stringed instruments the OMSP deals primarily with the problems of cello playing. It would be rather pretentious to claim that violinists should adopt cello-playing principles. Rather, I maintain that coinciding principles, and there are many of them, should be observed by all. That is why the thinking process itself can be useful for all instrumentalists, and it has proven itself to be so.

Category IV: Musical Application

Eventually the OMSP turns its attention to the fourth group, musical application, for the sake of which all the previous subjects were explored. At an early phase of this discourse, which I am rather inclined to call a "Short Soundless Summary of the Starker String Seminars" (to practice alliteration), I indicated the implied cold-bloodedness in this approach to making music. May I suggest reading a recent bestseller with the thought-provoking title of *Zen and the Art of Motorcycle Maintenance,* by Robert M. Pirsig,[2] or at least the sixth chapter of that book. The author meditates:

> The romantic mode is primarily inspirational, imaginative, creative, intuitive. Feelings rather than facts predominate. . . . The classic mode, by contrast, proceeds by reason and by laws—which are themselves underlying forms of thought and behavior. . . . Although surface ugliness is often found in the classic mode of understanding it is not inherent in it. There is a classic esthetic which romantics often miss because of its subtlety. The classic style is straightforward, unadorned, unemotional, economical and carefully proportioned. Its purpose is not to inspire

2. New York: William Morrow, 1974.

emotionally, but to bring order out of chaos and make the unknown known. It is not an esthetically free and natural style. It is esthetically restrained. Everything is under control. Its value is measured in terms of the skill with which this control is maintained.

To a romantic this classic mode often appears dull, awkward and ugly, like mechanical maintenance itself. Everything is in terms of pieces and parts and components and relationships. Nothing is figured out until it's run through the computer a dozen times. Everything's got to be measured and proved. Oppressive. Heavy. Endlessly grey. The death force.

Within the classic mode, however, the romantic has some appearances of his own. Frivolous, irrational, erratic, untrustworthy, interested primarily in pleasure-seeking. Shallow. Of no substance.

These excerpts may explain to the reader that my attempt is to combine the romantic and the classic modes in dealing with the "skill" part of our art.

> The "motorcycle," so described, is almost impossible to understand unless you already know how one works.

This sentence may explain the omission of charts, musical examples, and pictures that would be called for in any attempt that deals with mechanical data. I am fully aware that in this chapter I have given only superficial treatment to many complex issues, but I expect the reader to be familiar with these matters and visualize, when necessary, the proposed solutions or training processes. This same expectation allows me to use only a few perfunctory references to the subjects discussed in the fourth group.

The OMSP, when presented in a seminar group, invariably combines with the standard, stereotyped master classes; master classes where the "master teacher–performer," after having listened to the young inexperienced player, suggests alternate ways of playing a piece, and usually demonstrates his ideas as well. These ideas are the result of a lifelong stage or studio experience, of a lifelong experience of playing and listening to the literature of Bach, Mozart, Beethoven, etc., and of forming musical stylistic preferences based on total exposure to life and music. To my mind the effect of these "end results" is of limited use to a young musician, or to a musician who may or may not ever have similar exposures. What may be of use is learning the means through which his or her individual gifts and experiences will be able to surface, or communicate.

With these principles in mind the fourth group is reserved for aspects of music making such as "sense of rhythm" versus "rhythmic sense" (pulse). As an exercise, beat with alternate feet while playing. Stress the direction of the beat and make the body follow it: a downward motion for the downbeat; an upward motion for the upbeat. Attention must be paid to the significance of constantly changing units. 4/4 bars may have one, two, or four units in them. Several bars may constitute one unit. The importance of every note, short or long, must be stressed. Tempo considerations must be based on audibility and singing quality of the shortest note. Failure to observe this can result in a tempo that is too fast, or one that lacks motion and so produces dullness. Contrasting moods and contrasting dynamics are of maximum importance; so are the visual, aural, and digital memorization whether or not one is using music. The use of visual imagery in the style and mood of the music, in order to reproduce the wished-for concepts at will, is also of paramount importance.

EPILOGUE

Just as the length of the discussion of the musical and artistic aspects of string playing is determined by the time available in any given gathering, so must this discourse be terminated by space limitations. To anyone who wishes to find truly scientific data concerning most of the subjects mentioned above, I suggest reading Gerhard Mantel's recent book, *Cello Technique*.[3]

To learn musical truth one has to spend one's life listening and playing as much as is humanly possible. Let us remember that string playing is significant, but it is only a part of music; and music is only a part of man's attempt to satisfy his aesthetic needs after his basic need of survival has been realized. First one has to answer one's own requirements, and then, one hopes, enrich the lives of others. I consider myself fortunate, as my needs have been answered. I hope I have assisted you in finding some answers to yours. This is the basic credo of OMSP.

3. Bloomington: Indiana University Press, 1975.

Helga Ulsamer Winold

Musical Aspects of Motion Analysis

INTRODUCTION

Once in a while it happens: we feel as if we are playing in a dream. Everything we want to express is projected, and our technique functions with ease and elegance as a display in itself or as a means of making the language of music understood. Then there are other times when we struggle through a piece, "making it a success," and, if we are lucky, nobody notices the great effort it took.

All the complexities that enter into a performance—health, mental disposition, muscular readiness, musical knowledge, feedback and control, and the desire to express—are finally executed by two hands and ten fingers that are set in motion. Psychologists struggle to explain how a skill can be performed and controlled at the same time, when we are anticipating not only the musical architecture of a piece but also the intermittent execution of each part of it, of every motion involved.

Different schools of thought have different solutions for many aspects of the execution of motions in string playing. That, however, is not my principal concern. I would like to discuss the initiation of a motion. Jesse Owens, the Olympic runner, is supposed to have said, "I lift my feet and God puts them down." If I give the right impetus at the time of the impulse, the continuation and the success of the motion will be the necessary outcome.

Music making is thought and emotion translated into movements that are as varied as there are variables in music. The problem I am concerned with is the grouping of separately initiated movements into one continuous motion that can be initiated by a single impulse. This single impulse for a compound motion results in fluency and

156

speed of string playing because entire patterns of movements will respond easily to the motor memory.

MOTION IMPULSES

The motion impulse is a command from the brain to move certain muscle groups. The muscular impulse is transferred to the fingers through moving joints. The shoulder muscle group gives the impulse for rotating the whole arm. The upper arm muscle group controls the forearm in two ways: extension and contraction, and rotation around its axis. The forearm muscle group controls the wrist, the hand, and the fingers. The initiation of the motion is important because it determines the outcome. The audible result can only tell us if it was successful or not.

A motion can be simple, that is, the motion impulse and the musical impulse coincide, as in the final strokes of the passage in Ex. 1.

Ex. 1. Dvořák, Concerto in B minor, Op. 104.

With the left hand on the string, the right-hand motion consists of two circles. The attack of the string occurs at the downward impetus of the circle, and the continuation of the circle prepares the next stroke.

A motion can be complex, as in the run in Ex. 2.

Ex. 2. Schumann, Concerto in A
minor, Op. 129.

Musically it is a single motion but it calls for many technical actions:
The fingers of the left hand move on the string, the forearm makes a
rolling movement, the arm transfers the fingers from one string to
the next and shifts to different positions. The right hand starts with
an accent, sets the bow in motion, crosses strings, increases
dynamics, and changes bows.

Exx. 1 and 2 each convey a single musical gesture. The multiplic-
ity of mechanical impulses of the second gesture should not detract
from the unity of its musical impulse. If the same impulse used in the
Dvořák example is used for each finger in the Schumann, the run will
never be fast enough, even if it is practiced at length. The player
must play many notes in one impulse, but the question is: how
many? what impulse? where and how?

The psychologist George Miller has pointed out that we can perceive and retain up to seven single items (letters or numbers) but that
we show much better retention when the bits or letters are grouped
into words.[1] The complexity of a word is analogous to a pattern in
music; it is easier to perceive and process a pattern than many single
notes. Another psychological factor is reaction time, or the delay
that occurs between the stimulus and the initiation of the response.
If we perceive a stimulus for a group of notes, we eliminate the delay
that would occur if each individual note were singly initiated.

This leaves us with the task of recognizing patterns in music,
determining the appropriate motion, and analyzing the point from
which the motion gets its momentum. Each pattern has a musical
and rhythmical impulse that can be interpreted in different ways.
This will result in different movements initiated by different
impulses.

I will now turn to specific technical and musical examples. Left-
hand motions will be treated first, going from small movements, like
trills and position patterns, to shifts and combinations of movements. The discussion of right-hand motions will follow, ranging
from whole-arm arpeggiating movements to single strokes, combination bowings, and spiccato.

1. G. A. Miller, "The Magical Number Seven Plus or Minus Two: Some Limits on
Our Capacity for Processing Information," *Psychological Review*, 1956.

LEFT HAND

Trills

A trill consists of repeated finger lifting and striking. To avoid the tiresome lift–strike impulse for each pair of notes a rebounding action can be used that is comparable to the bounce of a drum stick on a drum: One impulse sets in motion a series of rebounds, which get weaker as the initial energy disappears. Shorter trills need only one impetus. For sustained trills the continuation of the impulse has to be lengthened with the least possible resistance in the arm and hand, or a new impulse has to be given periodically.

Patterns in one position

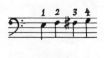

Ex. 3

The same impulse, resulting from the finger lift–strike action is used for patterns in one position. When playing the pattern shown in Ex. 3 slowly, each finger gets the same impulse from the preparatory lift. The arm weight moves from one finger to the next, and this weight transfer results in a slight rolling sensation from the inner to the outer part of the hand. As the pattern is sped up and repeated, the striking of the fourth finger coincides with the lifting of the first finger and the four single impulses (indicated by arrows) melt into one single one that gains additional momentum from the forearm rotation (Fig. 1).

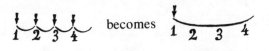

Fig. 1

When Ex. 4 is played slowly, each finger gets a single lift–strike impulse, but at a faster tempo we need to combine single notes into patterns that can be played with one impulse for several notes. We can divide the Beethoven excerpt into five units (Ex. 5), each of which can be played with one impulse. The impulse sets the hand in motion, and the momentum transfers the weight from finger to finger in a falling-domino effect.

Ex. 4.   Beethoven, Sonata in A major, Op. 69.

Ex. 5

Looking at the musical line and the tempo marking ¢ in Ex. 4, we may want to combine even more notes in one impulse: Finger patterns 1 and 2 repeat the same motion and can be played with one impetus for both. The change of direction in pattern 3 needs a new impulse that sets up the downward motion of the run (Ex. 6). Now the motion impulses coincide with the rhythmical impulses and the shape of the musical line. However, a performer may want to emphasize the fluency of the music and reduce the four impulses to only two, as in Ex. 7.

Ex. 6

Ex. 7

In reviewing the steps we have taken with this small excerpt, we see that we can find several musically and technically valid solutions. We can play the same two bars with six, four, or two impulses. If we use six impulses the phrase will sound loaded with energy, while it will float elegantly if we choose to play it with only two. The motor memory will react easily to a few impulses and we can avoid endless repetition of a series of single notes when practicing.

Shifts

We have discussed motion impulses resulting from finger lifting and striking and weight transfer by means of forearm rotation. For shifting we need new impulses because the motion is different.

The motion impulse for a shift consists of a chain of impulses originating in the rotation of the shoulder, which puts the arm into a different position. Simultaneously the forearm extends or contracts and changes the direction of the hand. The arrival of these impulses in the fingertips causes a weight release into a timed slide at the end of which the weight is put back into the fingertips. This sensation is comparable to the one a skier feels when he gets the impetus from a dip in the ground to carry him on weightlessly.

When we have ample time for shifting, as in a moderately slow melodic line, we can choose where to borrow the time for the slide, from the departure note or from the arrival note. If the two notes of the shift should not be connected by a slide, the shift should coincide with the phrase division of the music. Ex. 8 illustrates these three shifting possibilities. Shift 1 and shift 3 may be done by taking time either from the departure note or from the arrival note. Shift 2 should coincide with the phrase division.

Ex. 8.   Dvořák, Concerto in B minor, Op. 104.

Now let us examine shift 1 in greater detail. We may want to give the main musical impulse to the second note (g). This would result in a slide that takes time from the departure note (b), and the weight of the shifting impulse is felt toward the arrival note (g). The same shift may be executed differently if we feel the first note (b) as the main musical impulse out of which the second note grows. In this case we feel the arm weight on note b and the time for the slide is taken from the arrival note (g), where the hand arrives weightlessly.

In slow tempo the choice of the impulse is a question of taste and interpretation; in fast tempo it is a matter of necessity.

When we play scales, triads, or broken chords the impulse is usually given to the note preceding the shift. The striking of the finger provides the downward impetus that, as it rebounds, releases the weight in the direction of the shift. In fast tempo, however, we often have to play larger groups of notes with one impulse. Then the arm motion conducts a large motion impulse that encompasses several secondary shifting impulses.

In Ex. 9 it would be musically unacceptable to give the impulse toward the shift and thus stress the second note of every four-note pattern. The weight release impulse that has to be given on each first note not only results in the shift but also triggers the finger motion of the following three notes. In the sextuplet at the end of the measure a second impulse is needed, not for shifting or other technical reasons, but to bring out the rhythmical structure.

The previous solution would be acceptable if the basic pulse were eighth notes. But a look at the score shows that the music here moves in quarter and half notes. So the ideal solution may be the one in Ex. 10, in which the eighth-note impulses become secondary ones. One major impulse carries the arm through the first half of the bar, the next impulse sets up the motion for the upper positions of the third quarter, and the last two impulses emphasize the rhythmic change that sets up the long singing phrase in the following measures.

Ex. 9.   Haydn, Concerto in D major, Op. 101.

Ex. 10

These few examples make us aware of the importance and the variety of left-hand motion impulses. They may result in rebounds or weight transfer of the fingers in shifts or direction changes of the arm. Sometimes we need new energy for technical reasons and we have to give new impulses that will be imperceptible to the listener; and at other times the technical impulse will coincide with a musical accent. The timing and the energy we give to an impulse depends on the tempo, rhythm, and shape of each part of a piece of music.

THE RIGHT HAND

When we pedal a bicycle we do not push continuously throughout the turn of the wheel; we give only one downward impetus that will carry out the whole circle. The impulse is strongest at the point of initiation and loses energy as it continues. If we do not want it to stop completely we have to prepare for a new impulse while the momentum of the previous one is still carrying out the motion. Similarly, the motions of the right hand are directed by the whole arm through a chain of impulses from the shoulder joint into the fingers. Continuous bow strokes call for a circular arm motion with the shoulder joint as fulcrum for a whole-arm stroke. For smaller bow units on the upper half of the bow the elbow acts as fulcrum around which the forearm circles. The circular motions can revolve clockwise or counter clockwise.

In the discussion that follows we shall use arrows to indicate the direction of the motion (see Fig. 2) and the thickness of the line to indicate the amount of energy in a motion:

$$O\textdotaccent \qquad \textdotaccent O$$

clockwise   counter clockwise

Fig. 2

Arpeggios over three or four strings

It is the shoulder rotation that sets the whole arm into a half circular motion. The weight is transferred into the fingers and changes from the outer hand near the frog to the inner hand on the upper half of the bow.

In slow tempo we give one impulse to each up and down bow; in faster tempo one impetus carries the arm up and down, as in Ex. 11.

Ex. 11. Tchaikovsky, Rococo Variations, Op. 33.

String-crossings, two notes slurred

When we slur two notes on each bow, the arm forms two circles, but each circle has a different direction: The down-bow counter clockwise ꗉO , the up-bow clockwise Oꗉ. This change of direction makes it necessary to give two impulses. When we combine both circles into one continuous motion, they form a figure 8, lying on its side, played with one impulse for each downward motion (Fig. 3).

Fig. 3

The first four bars of Ex. 12 consist of six figure-8 movements that have the impulse for the downward motion on the outsides of the 8 (as in Fig. 3). At measure 5 the pattern and the motion change, and we need the impulse for the upward motion. It gets its momentum on the inner lines of the figure 8. This fact is often overlooked and results in a scramble.

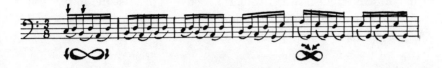

Ex. 12.   Bach, Gigue from Suite in C major.

Six or eight notes slurred across two strings

When we cross our legs and drop the crossed-over leg, we feel it bouncing up and down lightly until it stops. In much the same way we feel a rebounding sensation in the forearm when we suspend the upper arm, as if playing in the middle of the bow, and drop the forearm. This up-and-down, rebounding motion of the forearm can be combined with the horizontal drawing of the bow for slurred string-crossing.

Ex. 13.   Brahms, Sonata in F major, Op. 99.

With each new bow we give a new impulse that will set off a series of rebounds. The difficulty in Ex. 13 is the fading of energy with so many rebounds at a high dynamic level. It is advisable to use a new downward impulse on every beat of the measure.

Ex. 14.   Bach, Prelude from Suite in G major.

If we use one bow per half bar in Ex. 14, we have a combination of two motions: a half circle and slurred string-crossings. One impulse from the shoulder forms the half circle for the first five notes. The downward impulse of the forearm rebounds against the upper arm for the last three notes. The impetus for the last three notes acts at the same time as the pickup for the next half circle.

Single strokes on the string
We can conceptualize single strokes as three different ways to use motion impulses: (1) The martelé stroke calls for one impulse for each single note. The impulse is created by arm weight and thrust followed by a sudden release of weight resulting in an explosive attack. It comes to a complete stop where new energy is gathered for the next attack. (2) The détaché stroke also has one impulse for each note, but the bow is not stopped between strokes. It gains its momentum from the speed at each bow change when the arm swings into the new bow direction. (3) Legato playing could be defined as the avoidance of impulses, or as a continuous chain of preparing impulses.

Ex. 15.   Haydn, Concerto in D major, Op. 101.

A series of single strokes is directed by circular arm movements that are enlarged for string-crossings. If the circles change direction they need a new impulse, but for circles in the same direction one impulse is sufficient for a whole series. In Ex. 15, at the start of the 32nd notes we give an impulse to a clockwise circle for each pair of notes, and that sets off the series of circles in the same direction. The energy of the initial impulse flows out in the 16th note. The next impulse repeats this process but the circles revolve counter clockwise.

Single notes off the string
When we play spiccato in moderate tempo we use the whole arm like a pendulum, and this impulse makes the bow touch the string at the bottom part of the pendulum's half circle. In a faster tempo the

swinging back and forth of the arm starts the hand swinging from the wrist, and the up-bow rebounds without a separate impulse. In very fast tempo the arm motion becomes a shaking that sets off continuing circles in the wrist and fingers (see Ex. 16).

Ex. 16.   Valentini, Sonata in E major.

Spiccato bowing crossing strings has two components: the down-bow impulse with rebounding up-bow on the first and third 16th note, and the shoulder rotation impulses that carry the elbow down and up for the string-crossings. In fast tempo the down-bow impulses become a continuous swinging of the hand from the wrist and we are only aware of the shoulder motion that swings the elbow up and down in a half circle.

Thrown bow
The initial energy, the continuation and fading out of a motion impulse, becomes especially evident in the use of thrown bow. If not disturbed or resisted, a thrown bow will rebound and taper out like a thrown Ping-Pong ball.

The impulse for several notes in one bow direction is a simple drop–pull sideways motion; but the reversal of the bow direction while the bouncing continues requires careful thought. As we need a new impulse the arm has to be ready for the drop into the new bow direction, which means it has to be in up-bow direction in the air at the end of the down-bow and vice versa. We can gain additional impulse from the swing of the hand and wrist at each bow change.

We cannot practice this bowing very slowly, but we can divide it into its components, as shown in Fig. 4.

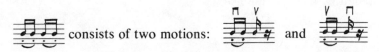

Fig. 4

The motion impulse at the beginning of the new bow has to be the same as the initial drop. The arm continues the motion during the rest.

Ex. 17. Dvořák, Concerto in B minor, Op. 104.

Similarly we can divide the bowing in Ex. 17 into its two components (Ex. 18). When each separate motion has gained the right impulse we let them continue themselves.

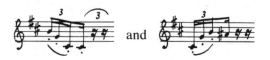

Ex. 18.

Just as left-hand technique involves a variety of motion impulses to meet various musical and technical requirements, right-hand technique demands an equally varied repertoire of motion impulses. If we play continuous strokes with circular arm motions the impulses depend on the size, speed, and direction of the circles. We can make use of the rebounding action of the forearm in an up-and-down bouncing motion or in a sideways reflex motion. The wrist, hand, and fingers receive impulses as a continuation of an arm motion, or they gain a momentum that lets them move independently at greater speeds. Each individual sound may require a different impulse depending on its articulation, length, dynamic level, and the context in which it occurs; or a whole series of sounds may be initiated by a single impulse.

CONCLUSION

Nobody would deny that an athlete has to find the most economical motions to achieve maximum accuracy with the least possible effort. And just like an athlete a musician has to find the most effective motions for the execution of his craft.

The performer has to have a clear perception of the piece of music he is performing. He has to know its style, form, rhythm, harmonies, and colors. In his mind he hears what he is about to perform, and his body perceives the impulse necessary for the musical execution.

A strongly motivated player will express what he desires to say with all available means. He might find the best solutions by intuition, or his strong motivation may carry him through unsolved difficulties. But if his performance lacks consistency, he needs to analyze the outcome.

The idea of looking for the right motion impulse may solve some problems or may inspire a new way of practicing. By forming motions that will make technical hurdles part of a congenial body feeling, we can turn nervous anxiety into musical excitement, or fluency and ease. Sometimes, however, we should add extra impulses to transmit the specifically called-for expression, because a piece of music should not necessarily sound effortless.

As one's mind grows to understand music one's body learns to find the most appropriate motions. Ideally the performer develops his sensitivity to music as he develops his technique to express it.

Tadeusz Wroński

Translated from the Polish by T. S. Robertson

A Plan for
Modernizing Violin Pedagogy

June 1978 marked the end of the twelfth year of my close association with the Indiana University School of Music. During this time I
have become familiar with both American education and musical life
in the United States. The newcomer from across the Atlantic meets
a situation here that is totally different from that on his own conti-
nent. He is alternately fascinated by the wealth of material equipment in music schools and the caliber of their faculties and shocked
by situations to which, initially, he cannot adjust. Gradually he
learns to understand the American lifestyle as well as the educational system, which for better or worse is an expression of the
needs and aspirations of this society. In the end, everything slowly
combines to form a logical picture in which many weaknesses turn
out to be only illusions and goals become clear.

It might seem that teaching the violin is the same in the United
States as in other countries. The personalities of the professors and
the talents of the students seem to exist in the same cooperative
relationship as in Europe, and the same esthetic ideals are guiding
lights for musicians all over the world. The final product of education is the same everywhere (regardless of the standard): a
high-caliber professional musician. Nevertheless, upon closer ob-
servation, it may be contended that in Europe there exists a certain
kind of continuity in music pedagogy. In the course of the last three
hundred years progressively better methods of teaching have developed, none of which appeared in a vacuum but rather were based on
the past, and none of which was the definitive method, but allowed
for evolution either through its continuation or through reaction
against it. National schools were established, flourished, and passed

away, and through the study abroad by students of a given national-
ity, a characteristic osmosis of ideas was achieved. Weak points
were overcome; new teaching approaches were sought. Nothing like
that exists in the United States. Here, outstanding individuals
achieve extraordinary results in teaching—and that is all. Perhaps
that is a great deal, especially since the number of such outstanding
musicians in the United States is probably the greatest in the world.
Nevertheless, these individuals live in the isolation of their own
class. Even their influence on other circles in their own music school
is slight, and then only through their students' performances. That
other, less prominent teachers benefit from this seems doubtful to
me. Influence outside one's own state does not exist at all. Individual schools have no contact with one another, nor is there any
exchange of ideas between centers of musical life and music
education.

Carl Flesch's *The Art of Violin Playing* influenced the standard of
teaching in all of Europe. When Flesch's adversary, Siegfried
Eberhardt, published his interesting series of books on violin playing, aspects of his thought supplemented Flesch's rather mechanis-
tic approach to teaching. Then before World War I Friedrich
Steinhausen's *Physiology of Bowing* appeared. That book was the
beginning of a modern approach to the teaching of the violin, and not
only in relation to the right hand. I will not elaborate here on the
succession of minor authors of methodological works, like
Trendelenburg, von der Hoya, Blobel, Jarosy, and Jahn, whose significance is of no comparison to the triumvirate of Flesch–
Steinhausen–Eberhardt. Among more recent authors, the works of
Jampolski and Mostras (Russian) and Feliński (Polish) truly open
new perspectives for the music teacher. In addition to the contribu-
tions of musicians, the research of other scholars, for example,
Nikolaj Garbusow (*Zonal Nature of Musical Pitch*), has enormous
importance for understanding the nature of good intonation in playing stringed instruments.

In Europe—either because educated people are more familiar
with foreign languages or because methodological works have been
translated into various languages—modern works on violin playing
are widely known. In America they are unknown. Flesch's works
are, of course, translated into English, but practically no one reads

them and no one encourages their reading. As far as I know, Steinhausen, Eberhardt, and others are still awaiting translation into English. Even if they were to be translated, that would not guarantee that they would be known, for several reasons. The first is that the programs of music schools do not include courses on the methodology of teaching instruments. The second is the fact that the teacher spends about one hour a week with each student; this, coupled with the demands of teaching (recitals), means that he does not have sufficient time to acquaint the student with the fine points of the methodology of playing or teaching. There is not even time to teach the student *how* he should work, how to develop his talent, how to shape his musical memory, how to conquer his stage fright, how to correct the faulty functioning of his hands, how to dislodge his psychological blocks. We barely have time to prepare the pieces to be played for recitals. Teachers have even less time for regular meetings on pedagogical or curriculum problems. Such meetings do not take place at all, and, furthermore, would probably not meet with general approval. We are all overworked to a degree unknown in other university fields, and we must confine ourselves to doing only the essentials.

If we were to look for what is typically American in the structure of music education, we would find it in the Bachelor of Music Education program. It is not my particular partiality to teaching at this level that causes me to confine myself to that subject here. My reasons for choosing this topic are twofold: first, this program is unique and has no exact counterpart in European education; and second, certain shortcomings of American music education in general can be seen most easily in the context of the program leading to the degree of Bachelor of Music Education. These deficiencies pose less of a problem in the programs leading to the Bachelor of Music or Master of Music degrees.

I do not know whether Americans are aware of the striking differences between their B.M.E. students and students in the education departments of European schools. The latter are those who are not sufficiently talented for performance careers, and therefore the playing demands are very low, something on the level of students who study music as an elective in American schools. At most, the graduate of the education department in Europe must be able to conduct music classes in secondary schools, lead the school choir, occasionally conduct a small instrumental group, teach classes in music appreciation—and that is all. In the United States, in thousands of schools, in thousands of small towns and locales, the graduate with the B.M.E. degree must know how to do all that we demand of a first-rate musician: teach *all* the instruments, conduct the school orchestra, teach theory, and, in a word, be a versatile musician of considerable ability. The requirements for the major field (the violin, for example) are high. The graduate must be able to play on performance level the concertos of Mozart or Bruch, or, what is even more difficult, the sonatas of Beethoven or Brahms. It is evident that the American B.M.E. program is a difficult one, and at the same time, socially important, for upon it primarily depends the musical education of society.

Thus the teacher of the B.M.E. student is presented with a very responsible task. He is given a student who is, on the average, less naturally gifted for performance but more overworked than the others because he must learn to play all the instruments as well as study a wide range of theoretical subjects. Very little time remains for work on his major instrument, yet the requirements of the Senior Recital are high. His intellectual development must be superior to that of the more narrowly specialized Bachelor of Music student. The graduate with the B.M.E. degree may face very difficult times: through his hands will pass not only hundreds of children playing just for pleasure and to earn credit hours at the secondary level, but often outstanding talents that he must know to guide without ruining them. It is clear that students in the B.M.E. program must be trained with particular clearsightedness, trained all-round, and trained with modern methods. B.M.E. graduates must know how to "set" the playing of their young students so that gifted pupils do not break down later in their development as a result of "unphysiological" playing that has been instilled in them, or during the inevitable corrections that will be necessary when they are in the hands of more experienced teachers. When a student for the B.M.E. arrives, we have four years to work with him. The starting point is relatively low, lower than that of B.M. students. Both the knowledge and the intuition of the professor are essential here, as well as appropriate *teaching materials*. Such materials, I contend, do not exist.

While the teaching materials available for training students in the B.M. and M.M. programs seem to me to be adequate, there is nothing at all with which to teach the students for the B.M.E. A regular student will practice isolated scales by Flesch or Ivan Galamian and various exercises by Ševčik, spend time on the collections of etudes by Dont or Gaviniés, and in later years possibly study the capriccios of Paganini or Wieniawski. He will work on progressively more difficult pieces and will, in the end, achieve professional competence on the violin. The B.M.E. student may, with great difficulty, make his way along the same road, but by playing too many etudes, he will waste time on works of limited musical value. The scales by Flesch and by Galamian are too complicated, and the jungle of Ševčik's exercises is frightening, so at most we explore it only occasionally. Paganini's and Wieniawski's capriccios are too difficult, while those by Gaviniés are too one-sided. The preclassical sonatas are excellent for developing musicality but cannot be played to the exclusion of other works, for the student will not progress technically. There are no collections of exercises introducing the student gradually to the problem of double-stops (those by Goby Eberhardt are not available today). The only exercises we have for shifting are in Ševčik's Op. 8; *Treffsicherheit auf der Violine* by Siegfried Eberhardt is a better collection for the same purpose, but it is not on the market. However, all these and the other exercises that we do have are intended for the development of the "general" student, the student who has time, who has a dozen or so years of work ahead. They are not suitable for the B.M.E. student, who:

is less talented than the B.M. student,
is less advanced,
has only four years for preparation,
has little time for practicing.

The materials we use to teach such students must be special ones; they must produce competence in playing in a way that is condensed, well thought out, and intensive. If these teaching materials are to include etudes, they should be selected ones. If they are to include scales, they should be simple and useful ones. If they are to include exercises, they ought to be only those that are proven and indispensable. Were we to have all this, such materials would still have to be provided with at least a brief systematic commentary and directions on how to practice them. Since they would be in a sense more intensive than "normal" exercises, it would be necessary to warn the student against forcing the hand and to provide simple instructions on averting this danger.

In order to create such materials, we need to familiarize ourselves with what has been done in other countries. There are, for example, the etudes by Joseph Kotek, of which Nos. 1 and 5 can be substituted for a hundred of Ševčik's exercises on shifting, and No. 6 is the best etude on double-stops that I know. Kargujev's exercises improve the strength of the hand with the utmost care. Siegfried Eberhardt's exercises for shifting and Goby Eberhardt's for double-stops are long out of print. The *Urstudien* by Flesch was conceived as exercise material for violinists who do not have a great deal of time for practicing. Another Flesch study, *Problems of Tone Production in Violin Playing,* treats exhaustively the problem of the so-called powerful tone on the violin. Maxim Jacobsen's *Paraphrases of the Kreutzer Etudes* is a source of many very interesting ideas for developing the technique of playing, and for the Paganini capriccios there is a small work by G. Mostras that is intended as an aid to mastering their difficulties.

An invaluable didactic work for students of the B.M.E. can be the Telemann fantasias for solo violin. Unfortunately, in the United States we have only the original text edition, an edition so faithful that it reproduces all the errors of the manuscript, even the omission of whole measures! To bring these fantasias within the reach of the student would require hours of work on the part of the teacher to supply sensible fingering. A good, practical edition by Eugenia Umińska has been published in Poland, but unfortunately it is very difficult to obtain in the United States. These fantasias are the natural step to the future study of the sonatas and partitas of Bach, but they are not used in the United States; thus B.M.E. students as well as B.M. students are forced to begin the study of the Bach sonatas and partitas from those works themselves. Pianists are better off, for a multitude of simpler Bach works are available to them before they begin work on *Das wohltemperierte Klavier.* We have only the fantasias of Telemann, and yet they are not available!

Besides the matter of availability, we face additional problems in the area of etudes. In the United States in particular, we generally use old, nineteenth-century editions, which contain antiquated fingering. We are always able to obtain the edition of the Bach sonatas done by Hellmesberger in 1865; and students generally play Bach in the Joachim edition dating from 1905. The 1924 Flesch edition is practically unused in the United States, and the most recent editions of the sonatas do not reach this country at all. This situation was at last rectified by the Galamian edition of 1971, but I suppose that it will take years before it replaces the less valuable, older editions on the market. The latter are much cheaper, for it is more profitable for publishers to reprint old editions than to set new ones by the leading modern specialists. Among the exceptions are the modern, well thought out editions by Josef Gingold and by Ivan Galamian, but they do not contain even a portion of the needed basic material. Another mistake on the part of publishing firms is the commissioning of new editions by famous soloists who are not teachers. The results of their work are interesting and give good insight into their own craftsmanship, but they are too difficult and complex and, in the main, are not suitable for students. Good editions can be done only by an outstanding instrumentalist and teacher with many years' experience, one who has been able to verify how his ideas and instrumental concepts are accepted by the average student.

In the last twenty years we have observed an essentially healthy movement toward more reliance on the authentic text without the accretions introduced by later editors. The goal is admirable and basically sound. Many European firms specialize in the publication of *Urtext* editions, but we must realize that they are not pure! Often they are supplied with a primitive fingering done by the publisher, and the composer is sometimes "corrected" in the matter of trills, grace notes, slurs, dynamics marks, or even particular notes. *Urtext* editions are generally published without commentaries, but where they are given, for example, in the Hauswald edition of the Bach sonatas, they contain everything except what might interest the performer. In a few places the notes in the manuscript differ from those in the *Urtext* edition, and in other places the authentic Bach text surprises musicians and evokes controversy. The decisions of the *Urtext* publisher in the Hauswald editions are not explained in the commentary; instead, it contains tables of discrepancies and differences among the various manuscripts and copies of the sonatas and partitas. Such a study is extremely detailed and scientific, but in a certain sense is of no value for the performer.

In his introduction Hauswald writes that he has not included in the text any "aids for performance" (fingering, bowings, dynamics marks) because they are superfluous for advanced violinists, who alone will be playing these works. How mistaken an approach! No student will be able to solve such problems alone. If the teacher solves them for him, the teacher will be compelled to do an enormous amount of work on the fingering and bowing of the *Urtext*, a host of things in the end superficial and based only on the principle, "I played it with such-and-such bowing and fingering." I worked for six years on my own edition of Bach's sonatas and partitas. In the second edition, a few years later, I introduced dozens of corrections and improvements that had occurred to me while working with my students, corrections prompted by problems that my earlier treatment had caused them. I mention this fact as proof of the difficulty and responsibility of producing a practical edition, even one based on the *Urtext*. It is precisely the students in the B.M.E. program who need the best possible editions. Perhaps they might be less essential if the program leading to the B.M.E. (and other programs as well) included courses on *fingering for the violin*. At present, no program at any music school contains this subject.

Thus, on the American sheet music market we have access primarily to obsolete editions (i.e., the *Urtext*s, which are expensive and, practically speaking, very difficult to use) or to ultramodern ones. A very small percentage of publishers meet the needs of today's music education. Contact with new publishers established since the war, for example, in Poland, Hungary, Czechoslovakia, or Bulgaria, does not exist. There—not to mention the interesting publications in the USSR—might be found many elements that would greatly enrich the teaching of the violin in America, and be useful especially in the B.M.E. program.

Here we may summarize what seems to be needed when considering these problems:

1. creation of a basic collection or collections of exercises to develop violin technique;

2. translation and publication of basic works in the field of violin methodology;

3. reprinting of valuable violin exercises now out of print;

4. gradual publishing of preclassical works, and then others as well, complete with well thought out, contemporary fingerings and bowings;

5. publication of etudes and exercises from other countries, works that are unknown in the United States;

6. publication of a textbook that might be used as the basis of a future course, "Violin Fingering";

7. publication of a textbook on the methodology of violin playing—for without such a text it would be difficult to introduce this subject into the program of studies;

8. a critical description of a modern course of study for beginners, utilizing everything from the past that is good and discarding whatever is doubtful or outmoded.

Some of these points might demand the creative and even the collective work of many teachers. Some could be accomplished through reprints, others through co-publication with foreign firms.

When I first came to Indiana University, I marveled above all at the standards and competence of my colleagues. I am full of admiration for what they accomplish, for their results with students who are often not overly gifted. I became acquainted with their ideas through their publications (as in the case of Janos Starker) and their editions of musical works (e.g., those of Josef Gingold). In addition, every examination and every performance by my colleagues' students was an opportunity for me to gain insight into their teaching methods. Let it remain my secret how many technical and interpretative ideas I "stole" from them! Furthermore, I saw as typical of the school in Bloomington the ideal interpersonal relations among the professors and their mutual respect. Thus it was all the more surprising to me that until now they have not cooperated with respect to any of the eight needs listed above. It is also surprising that there has not been sufficient desire on the part of the faculty to establish at Indiana University a center of creative thought that would influence both the nation and the whole world.

I might employ an analogy here from the field of chemistry: in a solution of different salts and other chemical bonds, a crystal may suddenly form, perhaps because the solution has been shaken or because it has passed through a certain level of saturation. Is this the moment when such a "crystal" might appear in our "solution"? I think that it is, and that maybe only one additional element is missing: the interest of other university authorities and departments. An encouraging factor for the development of this project might be that music publishing is a very remunerative field. It seldom happens that all the ingredients combine so propitiously: a real need, qualified participants, and a profit-making venture! If we could produce even a portion of the materials necessary for the proper training of B.M.E. students, our work could serve, in principle, all students in all programs and improve the fundamentals of teaching in general. By confining our considerations to the problems of the B.M.E., we could establish the project's initial dimensions and determine our selection so that we might stick to what is essential. It would help us simplify the content, avoid diffuseness, and condense the material so that we eliminate subjects that might be interesting but not necessarily useful. We must not rule out what already exists, but in the case of the B.M.E. student, we must give him *everything* he needs, and for the B.M. or M.M. candidate we would provide the fastest possible access to those elements contained in already existing collections of exercises.

This goal in the education of string students must start somewhere and sometime. Perhaps it will be at Indiana University or one of the other fine music schools in the United States, but start it must. As a proud member of a great faculty I hope we will be one of the first schools to take these important steps.

Notes on the Contributors

JAMES BUSWELL IV was born in Ft. Wayne, Indiana. At the age of seven he made his violin debut with the New York Philharmonic. He studied with Ivan Galamian at Juilliard and was an undergraduate at Harvard. He has made solo appearances with nearly every major symphony orchestra in North America, is known as a recitalist and recording artist, and has participated in several Spoleto Festivals of Two Worlds. Professor Buswell is an artist–member of the Chamber Music Society of Lincoln Center and has been on the faculty of Indiana University since 1974.

JOSEF GINGOLD, Distinguished Professor of Music, was born in Russia in 1909 and emigrated to the United States in 1920. He studied the violin with Vladimir Graffman in New York and Eugene Ysaÿe in Belgium, and concertized in both Europe and the United States before embarking on his orchestral career. He has played in the NBC Symphony under Toscanini, and was concertmaster and soloist with the Detroit Symphony and the Cleveland Orchestra. Professor Gingold joined Indiana University in 1960. He has also conducted master classes in Tokyo and Paris, and is editor of thirty-five violin works.

MURRAY GRODNER is a native of New York City and holds degrees from the Manhattan School of Music. He has played in the New Opera Co.-Ballet Theatre orchestra, the Pittsburgh Symphony, the Houston Symphony, and the NBC Symphony. Professor Grodner joined the Indiana University faculty in 1955, and is one of the original members of the Baroque Chamber Players. He has participated in international string and double bass workshops and seminars in England, Switzerland, Australia, and Costa Rica, as well as in the United States.

FRANCO GULLI was born in Trieste, Italy, and began his violin studies with his father, who was a pupil of Ševčik's. He earned an Artist Diploma at the Music Conservatory of Trieste, and studied further with Arrigo Serato and with Joseph Szigeti. He was concertmaster of the Milan Chamber Orchestra and soloist with I Virtuosi di Roma, and has enjoyed a worldwide career as a soloist since 1958. Professor Gulli held posts at Accademia Chigiana in Siena and at the Conservatory of Lucerne before coming to Indiana University in 1972.

GEORGES JANZER, born in Budapest, began his musical education as a violin student at the Franz Liszt Academy. At age 19, he graduated from the Conservatoire de Musique in Geneva. He has concertized internationally and was concertmaster of the Budapest Symphony Orchestra. He is the violist of the Vegh Quartet, which won the Grand Prix du Disque, and of the Grumiaux Trio, which has also won many prizes for performances and recordings. Professor Janzer has taught viola at academies in Hannover and Düsseldorf and, since 1972, at Indiana University.

ALBERT LAZAN is a native of Worcester, Mass., and a graduate of the Juilliard School of Music, where he studied with Edouard Dethier. He has played with the Pittsburgh Symphony under Fritz Reiner and the Dallas Symphony under Antal Dorati. Professor Lazan joined Indiana University in 1948 and was a member of the Berkshire Quartet from 1948 to 1965. He is editor of Three Sonatas by Veracini and author of *Basic Violin for Adults*.

FRITZ MAGG began his musical studies in his native Vienna and continued them in Cologne and Berlin with Paul Grümmer and in Paris under Diran Alexanian. He became solo cellist of the Vienna Symphony and, later, in New York, of the orchestras of the New Friends of Music and the Metropolitan Opera. He was a member of the Gordon String Quartet and now plays in the Berkshire Quartet, with whom he joined Indiana University in 1948. In addition he has concertized widely in the United States and abroad.

LAURENCE SHAPIRO was born in Boston but grew up in El Paso, Texas. Through his teachers he can trace his pedagogical heritage to the legendary Carl Flesch, D. C. Dounis, and Leopold Auer. He has served as concertmaster and soloist with several American symphony orchestras, toured with the New York Baroque Ensemble, and was first violinist of the Delaware and the Evansville string quartets. In 1972 he gave a series of television lectures about chamber music. Professor Shapiro joined Indiana University and the Berkshire Quartet in 1976.

ABRAHAM SKERNICK, born in Brooklyn, N.Y., studied violin with John King Roosa and viola with Emanuel Vardi and Nicolas Moldavan. He has been solo violist of several American symphony orchestras, most notably the Cleveland Orchestra, where he occupied that position from 1949 to 1976. He was the violist of the Mischakoff and the Cleveland Orchestra string quartets and has taught viola and chamber music at Peabody Conservatory, Oberlin Conservatory, and the Cleveland Institute of Music. In 1976 Professor Skernick joined Indiana University and the Berkshire Quartet.

JANOS STARKER, Distinguished Professor of Music, was born in Budapest and was graduated from the Franz Liszt Academy. He was solo cellist with the Budapest Opera and Philharmonic, the Dallas Symphony, the Metropolitan Opera, and the Chicago Symphony orchestras. An internationally known soloist, lecturer, and recording artist, Professor Starker won the Grand Prix du Disque in 1948 and was awarded honorary doctorates of music by Chicago Conservatory College in 1961 and Cornell College in 1978. He has been associated with Indiana University since 1958.

HELGA ULSAMER WINOLD was born in Munich and studied with Adolf Steiner and André Navarra. She earned her Bachelor's and Master's degrees at Cologne Conservatory, and her doctorate at Indiana University, where she studied with Janos Starker. Her career has included appearances as soloist with symphony orchestras, solo and chamber-music recitals, and recording sessions in Europe and America. Professor Winold has conducted clinics in the United States and abroad, and since 1969 she has taught cello, cello literature, and chamber music at Indiana University.

TADEUSZ WROŃSKI was born in Warsaw and holds diplomas from the Warsaw Conservatory and the Royal Conservatory of Music in Brussels. He has performed throughout Europe (including the USSR), Asia, and North America and has received numerous awards for artistic and pedagogical creativity. Among his publications are performing editions of solo violin works by J. S. Bach and Paganini, and four volumes entitled *Problems of Violin Playing*. Professor Wroński has been professor and president of the Warsaw Conservatory, visiting professor at Indiana University from 1966, and a member of the permanent faculty since 1975.